"A captivating personal reflection of Ghannoum's early years waltzing with international trade, viewed now with the seasoned lens of experience and education that leaves the reader with lessons in multicultural leadership and a compass for their own journey inward."

- John A. Clendenin, Former Senior Faculty of Harvard Business School

"In this thrilling business autobiographical account, Ghannoum skillfully evokes the mystery and romance of the Silk Road and provides **timeless lessons for those who dare to follow in his footsteps.**"

- Daniel Whitehead, *The Wandering Grocer: A Trip Around the World in 1898*

"A compelling and witty account of the thrills of doing business on the Silk Road, an ancient region where old meets new, where the historical wine and silk trades return as dollar bananas and chicken broilers championed by modern corporations, all set against the backdrop of the complex geopolitics of the post-Cold War era."

- Michael Karam, *Tears of Bacchus: A History of Wine in the Arab World*

"A powerful journey of reflection, blending political, cultural, social and economic perspectives in equal measure in this profoundly human account of the Supply Chain. The essential importance of personal values and principles is constantly underlined and will leave a lasting impact on the reader."

- Jon Harris, The Chartered Institute of Logistics and Transport

D1228019

SUPPLY UNCHAINED

TRADE, TREACHERY AND TRANSFORMATION
ALONG THE SILK ROAD

AHMAD GHANNOUM

Jacket Design: Candice Davidian Benmore
First Edition, 2021
ISBN 978-1-7372880-2-2

For Raya, Mia & Ziyad

TABLE OF CONTENTS

PROLOGUE

We travel not for trafficking alone;
By hotter winds our fiery hearts are fanned:
For lust of knowing what should not be known
We take the Golden Road to Samarkand.

– James Elroy Flecker, The Golden Journey to Samarkand, 1913

4:15 AM: an awfully curious hour for a shoeshine. Even odder was the location, Bayrampaşa Hali—Istanbul's bustling wholesale fruit and vegetable bazaar. An expectant crowd of fruit peddlers gathering around the spectacle of my shoeshine was now approaching a dozen strong. Such were the circumstances in which I found myself, one cold, wet autumn morning in 1999 at the age of 21, on my first day of moving bananas through the *hal's* outlet No. 57.

"*Abi!*" I called out to a scruffy, elderly man as I pointed toward a polishing brush he had unwittingly dropped to the ground. He picked it up and proceeded to thank me, wearing a warm congenial smile that only a time-worn septuagenarian could pull off. I was perfectly happy to get back to my work, but the shoeshine man was having none of it—not before I was rewarded with a shine on the house.

"*Teşekkür ederim abi, problem yok.*" I was trying to shake him off with elementary Turkish—in part to get back to a growing queue of customers, in part because I was not prepared to burden this man, who was old enough to be my grandfather, with service. But my objections fell on deaf ears, and before I knew it, the horsehair was already doing its magic on my leather boots.

Once the routine was complete, I reciprocated by offering what loose change I had on me, which was met with another heartfelt smile as the old man—to the growing anticipation of the crowd—reached into his pocket and presented me with a modest red pepper barely the size of a grape. I took the pepper and prepared to swing it into my own pocket when he grabbed me by the arm.

"*Şimdi ye.*" I was to eat it now, he said. He suddenly wore a gaze that indicated a failure to do so would be a grave insult.

Just to end the standoff, and without giving the matter further thought, I proceeded to chew on the pepper whole. The observing crowd instantly burst into a fit of roaring laughter, and before the chili's pungent properties could express themselves fully in my mouth, I knew I had committed a fatal mistake.

All along—starting with the staged drop of the brush—I was being played for a fish. To these seasoned sharks at the Turkish bazaar, I was a rookie foreign elitist who thought he could use his college degrees to shed his green skin at their playground. Transitioning from outsider status to gaining the respect of these hardened men down at Bayrampaşa Hali would be long and painful.

So began my education in trade and supply.

There is a certain romance involved in supply: a glue that connects us all as goods trade hands between farmer, plant worker, logistics handler, and consumer. As cargo traverse borders and societies, it not only fulfills the needs of its procurer, but also enriches all that it touches along its route with the stowaway knowledge and ideas that come part and parcel with the journey.

To supply is to engage in the oldest dance. It is a dance that was reinvented with the advent of agriculture 15,000 years ago and choreographed to provide a raison d'être for collaboration and coexistence. It is also a dance that seldom delivers a dull moment, with a twist, turn or spin to be expected with every step.

To me, few of life's pleasures can match up to the sight of cargo in motion, be it the buzzing of forklifts across the aisles of a warehouse, a freight train pulling into a station, or a ship leaving port—her foghorns echoing over the open sea ahead. Every instance along the *chain* continues to send shivers down my spine twenty years after my induction into the world of supply. It is truly a thing of beauty.

In a sense, we are all born into this business of supply. My earliest recollection of an act of supply is probably my sweetest and takes me back to the summer of 1983. I was a vacationing 5-year-old kid and had just caught my first fish—a grey mullet, skillfully and sustainably sourced with a pole stick off the Old Harbor in Limassol, Cyprus. "How much tastier was it than all the other fish you've had in your life?" I asked my mother for the umpteenth time. I instinctively felt fulfilled to be on the provider side of the equation and was instantly hooked (not least on fishing).

A second memory from my formative years piqued my curiosity about the business and ethical ends of supply. My father, an airline pilot for the cargo carrier Trans Mediterranean Airways (TMA), was explaining to me that a flight delay had led to the culling of tens of thousands of day-old chicks. They had grown in the interim and now required more space, rendering their shipping by air a financially unfeasible transaction.

The story of the culled chicks stayed with me. Many years later, it would influence my decision to start my professional career by accepting a role that centered around the supply of poultry products (as well as bananas and other food commodities). Those subsequent experiences in my life—set along the ancient Silk Road that stretches from Turkey to Central Asia—provide the setting for this book. The events unfold against a backdrop of political and socioeconomic transition to the post-Cold War era.

Writing these pages arose from two lingering temptations.

The first was to share the empirical lessons that I gained from my experiences. It is my conviction that these lessons are universally applicable across industries, but especially to those operating within a framework of a turbulent and fast-evolving industry.

The second was to provide insights into the lives of the unsung heroes of the supply world. These are the people who work around the clock—supply does not stop—to ensure that there is fresh milk on the breakfast table every morning, or that wooden logs make it to the chimney by first snow.

I draw on personal experiences set as far and wide as the historic bazaars of Central Asia, the seaports along the Black Sea and the poultry plants of Brazil. I revisit pleasant encounters with individuals who opened their doors and hearts, but also the hardships of the sleep-deprived nights aboard a distant banana boat. Finally, I recollect the traumatic episodes that ended in the bodily harm—or worse—to colleagues on the job who fell victim to kidnap and even murder.

My professional education began on that early morning at the *hal*, my mouth burning, the crowd laughing and jeering at me. It was an intimidating experience, but a necessary one. Among thousands of tons of fruits and vegetables, I would live through and grow out of my salad days. At times, I would wonder whether the thundering rains, nauseating diesel trucks and veteran hagglers were not colluding against me. But to succeed in this business, I had to earn respect, and it was already becoming clear that morning how it was to be done. I had to stand my ground, think on my feet, acclimate to the prevailing mindset, and be willing to laugh—even at my own expense.

Furthermore, I had to be prepared to break bread with those men and to drink from the same unwashed tea glass that had brushed against a dozen unkempt moustaches. More importantly, I had to learn the language and differentiate the various dialects and customs. Finally, I was to sync my biological clock with the working hours of the fruit world. That is to say, I had to be up at 3 AM every morning and fast asleep by 9 PM.

If I could accomplish all that, only then could I hope to make an honest dollar selling bananas. For the rest of that Turkish autumn, I readied to do all that and more as I committed the bulk of my pre-dawn hours to Bayrampaşa Hali.

Equally, I had to succeed at the port. If there were an intimidation scale from 1 to 10, where a Turkish prison scored a perfect 10, Bayrampaşa Hali would stand at a respectable 7. The seaports, I was about to find out, deserved nothing short of a 9. It was at the ports that product arrived before making its way to the distribution facilities and on to the *hals*, supermarkets, and grocery stores. The ports at Gemlik and especially Mersin provided many a banana with access to Turkey and its neighboring countries to the east and northeast. If I were to really understand the intricacies of this business I was in, and to succeed, it was of the essence that I jump aboard the next banana boat and suffer the niner firsthand.

My plan, to get through it all, was to let myself fall in love with the trade and be consumed by an obsession for learning the undiscovered. It would be a love unrequited and best captured by the Lebanese poet Kahlil Gibran through the words the eponymous prophet speaks to the people of Orphalese. *"If in fear you would seek only love's peace and love's pleasure, then it is better for you that you cover your nakedness and pass out of love's threshing-floor, into the seasonless world where you shall laugh, but not all of your laughter, and weep, but not all of your tears."* I was prepared to laugh all of my laughter and to weep all of my tears.

Scanning the arrivals section of *Sopisco*, a newsletter dedicated exclusively to the banana trade, I set my sights on the *M/V Bolivar*, a reefer vessel that we would be receiving at the port of Mersin later that September to deliver her bounty of 1,700 tons of Ecuadorian Cavendish bananas. The city of Mersin, along the eastern Mediterranean, hosts what is in many ways the most strategically situated port in Turkey. It offers a gateway for transit supply routes in and out of the geographically confined regions of the Caucasus and Central Asia, as well as to the remote northernmost parts of Iraq and Iran. It also provides ships with an entryway to Turkey without having to fly their colors past the choking waterways of the Dardanelles and the Bosporus.

I reached out to Rabih Naboulsi, a childhood friend and future business partner, who agreed to make the coastal drive from Beirut, Lebanon to Mersin and help supervise the unloading of the *M/V Bolivar*. The discharge operation spanned 72 sleep-deprived hours, but it became apparent from the moment the seals came off the hatches that the scope of operations we faced was not something one learned at business school. Unloading a vessel was something one could learn only from experience. The undertaking proved to be less about moving boxes and pallets from the vessel onto trucks, and more about preventing fraud. In the supply world, commodities—be they bananas, coffee beans, or iron ore—are so liquid that the *M/V*

Bolivar may just as well have been unloading stacks of cash. Having her cargo stowed in break bulk (loaded inside the ship's hold in loose cases, as opposed to stacked in sealed containers) brought about a scene reminiscent of an all-you-can-grab buffet for hustlers.

At the port, a cat-and-mouse game ensued over the entire three days, as four parallel cranes hauled cargo back and forth toward expectant trucks lined up alongside the moored vessel. The extent and sophistication of fraud was such that Naboulsi and I were finding it impossible to maintain the integrity of the operation, which was now running at full speed. Vast quantities of bananas were consumed by gangs of stevedores inside the vessel's hatches, as evidenced by a stupendously thick layer of banana skins covering the floors of the emptied storage compartments. Many stevedores wore especially adapted jackets lined with deep inside pockets that could hide up to 20 kg of bananas at a time. Others orchestrated the dumping of whole banana cases overboard, where conspiring gang members swung their steely longshoreman's hooks at the jettisoned cargo and lifted them aboard their stealthy dinghies under the cover of the moonless nights.

The truck drivers were not left out of the frenzy. Their most prevalent ploy was to carry steel shafts, representing 10 or 15 percent of a trailer's weight, through the weighbridge at the port's entrance, only to dump the ballasts once inside the premises and compensate for the unaccounted weight with *contrabanda*. Amidst this flurry of activity, one could be forgiven for believing bananas were vanishing into thin air.

To add insult to injury, Naboulsi and I—playing the role of vigilant cops—would be personally targeted through pressure tactics that ranged from feigned disobedience to the disappearance of the jackets that kept the cold out at night. Even our meals would frequently vanish.

"Where's my cheese?" I once called out to a port associate, whom I worked hard to befriend.

"You ate it all," he said blithely. "What's the matter with you?"

It was a load of bunkum, of course. But I had neither the energy nor the time to spare processing a thought on processed cheese.

The hardest part to deal with was that many large corporations tolerated all this fraud—and worse—as a cost of doing business. I would later learn of the power wielded by stevedore syndicates and unions the world over who were not above shutting down ports to get their own ways, with precedents set at ports as prominent as those in New York, Rotterdam, and Marseille.

Ultimately, the discharge of the *M/V Bolivar* did not go as I had planned. Yet it became the moment that defined the start of my career: my initiation to the realities of the business world. While the experience did not immediately yield dividends, the lessons I learned would later provide a foundation for completely overhauling our unloading operations—and in time, generate hundreds of thousands of dollars in savings when our ships called at Mersin, Constanța, and Poti. I took a beating, but it was with love... as prescribed by Kahlil Gibran.

After the *hal* and the port, I completed my induction to the business of supply by serving time at the distribution centers that housed the storage and handling units for our products, including Cavendish bananas. Once cargo was discharged from the vessel and loaded onto trucks, it was delivered to these distribution centers. Product was received, allocated storage space, and handled, as needed, until it was ready for dispatch to a customer or a sales outlet.

It is hard to imagine a fussier product than the Cavendish banana. It must be stored at precise temperatures and ripened via an extremely delicate procedure. The Cavendish tolerates no other fruit in its vicinity, lest it diminish its longevity and the other qualities associated with its taste. By spending time at our partner Dole's state-of-the-art reefer facility in Istanbul—the largest of its kind in continental Europe at the time—I learned everything there was to know about bananas, including the fact that a banana remains a living being long after it has been harvested; a being that rewards its purveyor handsomely when treated with care and respect, but one that could just as easily drive them to ruin at the hint of a disturbance.

SECTION ONE
MOVING PRODUCT

It is better to be lucky. But I would rather be exact. Then when luck comes you are ready.

– Ernest Hemingway, *The Old Man and the Sea*, 1952

CHAPTER ONE
DEPREM!

It was the morning of August 17, 1999, and the landline at my home in Beirut was ringing nonstop. Worried relatives and friends were frantic for news. Was I safe at home, or was I close to the epicenter? Did I survive it, or was I swallowed under the rubble?

Survive what?

Earlier that morning, it turned out, Turkey had been rocked by one of the deadliest earthquakes in living memory. The brunt of the devastation was suffered by the densely populated city of Izmit, to which geologists traced the epicenter of the quake—measuring 7.6 on the Richter scale. Over the next few days, the scope of devastation would unfold through blaring television screens with the number of fatalities revised by the hour from 800 to 5,000, and ultimately, to 15,000. That official tally, of course, failed to account for another 30,000 individuals who were registered as missing, never to be found. The quake would leave many more displaced, with estimates of the number of people losing their homes ranging between 250,000 and 500,000.

But the scale of the damage was not all nature's doing. Later investigations into the abnormally high death toll and the scale at which entire blocks had collapsed to the ground pointed to corruption. Rampant decay in the system had infected the realms of property developers and municipal inspectors, resulting in lax compliance to construction codes and the overcrowding of buildings erected on poorly consolidated land.

In the aftermath of the quake, heads rolled in both the public and private sectors. The economy regressed, banks went bust, and the Turkish lira devalued at an alarming rate. A growing economy thus abruptly stopped dead in its tracks, and over the following year, the financial meltdown sent the Turkish lira further tumbling with hyperinflation hitting 70 percent. Although not an entirely new phenomenon in Turkey, this round would prove acute enough to help the lira reclaim its *Guinness Book of World Records* title as the world's least valuable currency. By the end of 2003, the Grand National Assembly of Turkey would drop six zeros off every banknote. A 1,000,000-Turkish lira bill, barely equivalent to a dollar, would be replaced by the simpler 1 new Turkish lira denomination.

The fallout of the quake had unmasked enough rot and corruption to cause another seismic shift, this time in the political landscape. That shift would culminate in the arrival of Recep Tayyip Erdoğan's *AK Parti* to power in 2002.

According to my original travel itinerary, I was supposed to take off for Istanbul barely three hours after the earthquake struck. Fresh out of the American University of Beirut (AUB), I longed to move there and join the ranks of entrepreneurs seeking to revive the heyday of trade along the ancient Silk Road. Following the collapse of the Soviet Union, the markets dotting Central Asia and the Caucasus were observing a new dawn of liberalized trade. Turkey's geographic proximity to these markets—as well as those emerging from communism in Eastern Europe—made it the ideal steppingstone into the neighborhood.

My initial intention had been to move on and settle in Azerbaijan, one of the most promising markets in the Caucasus—owing to massive oil and gas reserves. Soon enough, I found that Istanbul was a much more advantageous logistical launchpad from which to cover the entire region. I would stay in Istanbul for much of my Silk Road adventure, dealing primarily in fresh bananas and frozen poultry meats.

Istanbul was just 70 km to the west of the quake's epicenter, as the crow flies, and the city suffered its fair share of devastation. But while I did dodge the tremor, there was no escaping its wide-ranging reverberations. As I set out to make the city my home for the next six years, I found the mood so skittish that the slightest of provocations triggered anxiety and panic in those around me. Aftershocks were a daily occurrence, each rekindling fears and tears among those who had experienced the original quake. It was little wonder that my first Turkish word would be *deprem*, meaning earthquake.

CHAPTER TWO
BIRTH OF A VENTURE

The year of my arrival in Istanbul was the year Thomas Friedman published *The Lexus and the Olive Tree*, a book heralding a new age of globalization to fill the gap left by the Cold War. It was also the year the James Bond movie *The World Is Not Enough* hit the cinemas with scenes set in Turkey, Azerbaijan, and Kazakhstan. In the film, the antagonist Elektra King builds the aptly named King Pipeline, which passes through the Caucasus and is modeled on the real-life Baku-Tbilisi-Ceyhan pipeline that promised to drive economic growth in the region. Together, Friedman's book and the latest release in the Bond franchise captured the scene nicely, portraying with remarkable accuracy the prevailing theme of the hour: a concoction of action, geopolitical drama, and financial windfall.

The opportunity to be a part of all that had me feeling like a giddy child holding a MaxPass for a Disney adventure park. I was never one for the beaten track, and the appeal of being among the pioneers reinventing the Silk Road excited me beyond words. The adventure of selling highly perishable products in emerging markets carried business and security risks considered extreme by most standards. But it was—and still is—my belief that where faith and dedication to the cause are steadfast, the risks can be managed to yield sizable rewards.

The door was now open for me to step into this brave new world. The person who opened that door was a gentleman called Fadi Nahas.

My earliest memory of Nahas was at one of the Ecuador Night events that he hosted as the Honorary Consul General of Ecuador in Istanbul. The parties served to promote the South American nation's interests in Turkey. They also afforded Nahas opportunities to strengthen personal relationships with figures who wielded some level of influence over how the fruit and meat trades—in which he was a major player—evolved in the region.

As always, it was a lavish evening with all the hallmarks of a vibrant South American carnival. Latin music and dance, fruit cocktail stands, resplendent feathers, and Panama hats—stowaways from an Ecuadorian banana boat—were on full display. But there was one feature to the party that was too far removed from the Latino scene to be missed, and it was standing right next to the exuberant Nahas at the main reception area: a donkey, draped for the occasion in an alpaca wool poncho.

"Who's the VIP?" I teased, as we traded niceties.

"Meet my hero!" he said, giving the beast a gentle tug by the rope. "Here's someone who's never made the same mistake twice." Nahas was sipping on his beverage of choice—a Diet Coke served in an oversized glass, *full ice*.

"Far out," I replied, my mind drifting toward what significance his words held. Nahas was a man at the peak of his business success. Somewhere down that road, it was inevitable that he must have erred. It now sounded like he was committed to avoiding a repeat of those mistakes.

The *donkey doctrine*—never making the same mistake twice—was something Nahas took to heart from an early age. As a result, donkeys would always hold a special place in his heart. I later learned that he once rescued a stray donkey that was caught in a blizzard in the mountainous town of Bsharri—birthplace of Kahlil Gibran and home to the biblical Cedars of Lebanon. Nahas not only paid to treat the donkey's broken leg, but also endeavored to find it a new life purpose by arranging for an apprenticeship at a traveling circus. On another occasion, he hired a crane to lift a donkey to his office for use as a prop for a motivational speech. It was vintage Nahas: spontaneous, eccentric, and fun.

Nahas had begun his professional journey working for businessman Costa Bitar in 1980s war-torn Lebanon. Bitar, owner of a reputed maritime shipping firm, came to play a big role in Nahas' life after the latter lost his father at an early age. Nahas idolized Bitar and strove to learn from him the core principles required for building and managing a business.

By the mid-80s, Nahas was ready to break out on his own. He was grubstaked the seed capital by Bitar to experiment with several startups, including an operation to supply Lebanon with Dole bananas. Banana distribution would prove profitable, but also cash intensive. Additional investors would be required, as would political and security arrangements to enable expansion across Lebanon—a geography that was increasingly fragmented because of the Civil War. Nahas soon found himself walking a tightrope when plans to expand the business failed to turn an immediate profit for his new associates. The line separating financing and security became increasingly blurry and Nahas was thrust into the eye of a perfect storm.

Around this time, Turkey—just 250 km from Lebanon's northern border—was at the final stages of negotiating its accession to the World Trade Organization (WTO). The conclusion of a deal would be a watershed moment for a nation intent on modernizing its economy and meeting a key prerequisite to joining the European Union as a member state. On the ground, accession to the WTO meant that Turkey's ports and border crossings would be open to free trade. Restrictions on the import of commodities, including bananas, were soon to be lifted, providing a unique opportunity to whomever could secure a reliable stream of supply.

Nahas saw that the opportunity to supply bananas to Turkey, a market 20 times the size of Lebanon, could provide the antidote to a difficult situation. He had to overcome two hurdles to seize upon it. The first was to find a local partner who could show him the ropes in Turkey. The second was to convince Dole—with whom he already had a working relationship in Lebanon—that he was the right man for the job.

The answer to the Turkish partner hurdle came in the form of Abdo Deletioğlu, a small-scale dealer of Turkish produce. Interestingly, it was Deletioğlu who showed up at Nahas' front door, not the other way around. When one of Deletioğlu's trailers made a delivery to Lebanon, as was frequently the case, it often backhauled Nahas' bananas to avoid making the return leg to Turkey empty—a journey that was almost as costly as it would be if the trailer were fully loaded.

The bananas turned a handsome profit for Deletioğlu, who had been pitching Nahas on the idea of a partnership to distribute bananas in Turkey for a while. Deletioğlu, who hailed from the Arabic-speaking city of Adana, would provide a fledgling infrastructure on the ground that the pair could expand. Nahas would complement

Deletioğlu by providing the level of business sophistication required for managing a relationship with a corporation of Dole's caliber.

It was not until 1989, when Turkey's membership to the WTO was sealed, that Nahas would finally take Deletioğlu up on his offer. But there was one more hurdle to overcome: a hiccup in Nahas' relationship with Dole, who was now concerned about his predicament in Lebanon.

Dole was not the only supplier with an interest in Turkey's virgin market. Franco Cortesi, the president of Chiquita in Italy, was actively scouring the scene for a distributor of his own. By a freak of fate, he found that distributor when he was seated next to Nahas on a flight from Beirut to Milan, Italy.

Nahas was blessed with unmatched charisma and an animated communication style that he could deliver in five languages, including Cortesi's native Italian. He pitched his Turkey plans to Cortesi, who took an immediate liking to Nahas and offered to supply a first trial shipment to Turkey on credit.

Nahas was taken aback by the immediate faith Cortesi was putting in him. He had to ask. "How can you provide someone you barely just met with a boatload of bananas and no payment guarantees?"

The experienced Cortesi peered back at Nahas, who was barely 30 years old at the time. "You strike me as a smart kid," he began. "In our industry, smart kids know that playing it straight is infinitely more profitable in the long run."

Just like that, the last hurdle along the road to Turkey was cleared. Often in life, it only takes one person to believe in you. For Nahas, at that point in his life, that person was Franco Cortesi.

The first vessel to carry imported Cavendish bananas to Turkey called at the port of Mersin later that year, heralding the coming of age of a young entrepreneur. Several shipments followed, but Chiquita's supply constraints would not be able to keep up with an explosion of demand as Nahas and Deletioğlu's distribution lines grew to cover Turkey's major cities.

This early success provided a proof-of-concept that Turkey was indeed open for business. It also offered Nahas with an opportunity to rectify his standing toward Dole—the only supplier capable of catering to Turkey's demands in full at the time—who was now prepared to enter the Turkish market with Nahas on his terms.

But Nahas would maintain his relationship with Cortesi. A ban introduced on the importation of bananas to Turkey over a decade later, coupled with an unfavorable ruling on a lingering trade war between the US and the EU, would cause Dole to partially lose its appetite for supplying product to Turkey. It was during that time that Nahas reconnected with Cortesi to establish alternative supply lines.

Through it all, there was a sustained market leadership position in Turkey, which would be leveraged to expand west to Romania and Moldova, and later east to the Caucasus and Central Asia. Additional partnerships were later forged with global food giants for the supply of other items—primarily frozen poultry products—that could benefit from a slight modification to the existing cold chain infrastructure. The most prominent of those partnerships took the form of joint ventures with Tyson Foods, Sadia, and AJC. Bananas and frozen poultry became the staples on which the venture grew.

To fuel growth, Nahas adopted a partnership-based model from the start. He appreciated that people were the beating heart of any organization; to attract a specific breed of entrepreneurial-minded professionals who were both talented and tolerant of hardships, he was prepared to share in the equity and profits of the venture. As a result, a complex network of ownership proliferated as profit centers sprouted across verticals and geographies. For someone of my profile—and there were a few—the model served to further fan our fiery hearts.

CHAPTER THREE
WISDOM ABOARD THE *HIAWATHA*

In Turkey, I began to cultivate an understanding of the nature of markets. They do not operate in a vacuum. Socioeconomic and technological forces shape supply and demand over time. Shifting consumer tastes can just as easily lift a firm's fortune as disruptive technology can bring it to its knees. These forces are often cited as external and outside an enterprise's direct control, but one can argue that a proactive enterprise has several levers at its disposal to both influence the trajectory of external trends and adapt to remain relevant.

Enterprises also contend with a third formidable force, one that I have come to believe supersedes even socioeconomics and transformative technology: that of geopolitics. Large organizations are always wrestling to shape the geopolitical landscape to their advantage by lobbying governments, influencing the media narrative, and swaying national sentiments. Excelling in this regard can unlock the door for sustainable gains; blundering can put a firm out of business.

As the term implies, geopolitics is the science of politics and international relations as it relates to prominent geographic—or more accurately, topographic—features. In a business context, engaging in geopolitics means playing a variant of chess where the objective is not capturing the opposing side's king, but rather attaining *kingmaker* status. It is a game played over a board shaped by earth's shifting tectonic plates—exemplified by the earthquake along Izmit's North Anatolian Fault. Much of what I would learn in the frozen food and fresh fruit trade would emerge from events unfolding in a geopolitical context—specifically that of the reemergence of the Silk Road at the turn of the millennium.

Early on, I endeavored to learn on a more abstract level. Even as I juggled my time between Turkey's bustling *hals*, ports, and distribution centers, I made time to participate in a workshop held along the waters of the Bosporus at the Çırağan Palace Kempinski Istanbul in November of 1999. The workshop was attended by representatives of large multinational food companies, including our partners Dole and Sadia, as well as by our country managers, who were based across Eastern Europe, the Caucasus, and Central Asia. Also present were consultants and political analysts with deep insights into our industry and the region in which we operated. We were all gathered to chart a roadmap for securing our two most important activities: sourcing—which I would come to lead on behalf of our organization—and distribution.

On the sourcing side, the overarching objective was to develop a strategy to secure our international supply lines in industries where often no more than two or three credible suppliers operated. On the distribution side, our priority was to strengthen our security and political cover in the wake of the unlawful detention of one of our staff in the Republic of Georgia. We interpreted the arrest as a form of harassment aimed at pressuring us out of the burgeoning food distribution sector there.

The harassment of private businesses was not an entirely unusual phenomenon in the region. As our geographic and operational footprint gained prominence on the ground, we became increasingly visible on the radars of corrupt officials and criminal syndicates. In fact, the line separating the two was often a blurry one. The fruit and poultry protein trades were not only lucrative, but they were assumed to require only rudimentary technologies and skills—making for low barriers to entry. This combination of traits made us the target of racketeers across virtually every market in which we operated. A significant part of the workshop at the Çırağan was dedicated to preempting further security incidents and avoiding a repeat of the Georgia detention case.

On that front, our strategy was to leverage the fact that the bulk of our suppliers were American companies. This meant that we, by extension, represented untouchable American interests—a supposition that we would shout from the rooftops to deter further provocation.

To drive this point home, a cocktail reception was organized aboard a historic native American boat—the *Hiawatha*—on the final evening of the workshop. Owned by the US Consulate General in Istanbul, the *Hiawatha* was the only boat authorized to fly the US flag as it cruised along the Bosporus. Hosting the reception aboard the *Hiawatha* was a move designed to showcase the backing and support afforded us by US State Department figures in Turkey and the region.

On deck, it was Frank Sánchez, one of the advisers facilitating the workshop, who distilled and delivered the takeaways from the conference in a sagacious keynote that highlighted three geopolitical themes for the coming years. First, the Banana Wars, a metastasizing cross-Atlantic trade feud, offered rare opportunities and unique challenges for sustaining our banana supply lines.

Second, a growing protectionist sentiment in Turkey, gaining momentum in the wake of the Izmit earthquake, threatened our banana imports in favor of locally grown produce. Finally, the Baku-Tbilisi-Ceyhan pipeline, now in its late stages of construction, promised a regional economic boom once the oil and gas riches buried underneath a landlocked Caspian Sea were liberated. How our operating strategy—starting with the banana trade—interacted with those three themes that are routed in the geopolitics of supply is addressed in the next three chapters.

Fig. 1 Map of the greater region home to the Silk Road.

CHAPTER FOUR

THE BANANA WARS:
OPPORTUNITY AND CHALLENGE

The Banana Wars playing out between the United States and the European Union offer a highly instructive case study in the interplay of politics and business. Their reverberations could be felt far and wide, complicating supply proceedings across a host of geographies and sectors.

From our perspective as a regional fresh and frozen food distribution powerhouse, the stakes were especially high in Turkey, our largest market with a population of 80 million people—or roughly the size of Germany. Our single largest revenue generator in that market was the modest Cavendish banana at the center of the trade dispute, its distribution propelled by a complex web of distribution routes, reefer storage facilities, ripening houses, and sales points. It is ironic that a product so simple required a logistical scope so sophisticated.

Our share of the banana market in Turkey was close to 60 percent, and it was becoming increasingly more difficult to maintain a growth trajectory. Moving forward, we had two alternatives to choose between in pursuit of further expansion: focusing on a product diversification drive in Turkey or expanding our geographic presence into neighboring markets that were emerging from communism.

Eventually, it was geographic expansion on which we would build our growth strategy. Our decision was premised on the universal popularity of bananas. Generating more revenue per capita than most other food items, the banana remained the world's most sold fruit and the fourth most traded food staple overall, with industry revenues exceeding $8 billion annually. It therefore made more sense to aim for a large share of a banana market in untapped places like Armenia and Moldova than it did to compete for crumbs selling less popular items in Turkey's saturated market. Additionally, being the first to enter any new market would afford us a first-mover advantage that would make it easier to protect market share over time.

In the meantime, further west, the trade war waged on the European Union by the United States was shaping up to be the mother of all trade quarrels. Oddly enough, the bananas at the heart of the dispute were grown neither in the United States nor in the European Union; the plantations were scattered across Latin America—a testament to the warring sides' imperialist legacies. While access rights to the European Union's banana market was at the center of the dispute, the fallout resulted in trade sanctions that affected at least a dozen other industries. The impact also spilled over political boundaries, with the interests of more than a hundred nations beyond the United States and the European Union directly or indirectly impacted.

The saga of the Banana Wars begins in the years following WWII, when European countries conferred special privileges on former colonies in Africa, the Caribbean, and the Pacific—collectively referred to as ACP countries—to sell their bananas in Europe. By doing so, they largely cut Latin American growers such as Ecuador and Colombia—who were under the influence of large American corporations—out of the European equation. Although initially offered sporadically and subjectively, the special privileges were later streamlined at the Lomé Convention in 1975. With 71 participating ACP countries, the convention consolidated and institutionalized the privileges under one structured banana regime. This regime would later be adopted by the European Single Market upon the formation of the European Union in 1993.

Among the hallmarks of the banana regime was a system that gave special duty-free import rights and guaranteed volume quotas to the signatories of the Lomé Convention. To the dismay of American corporations—primarily Chiquita Brands International and Dole Food Company—the regime constrained the import of banana harvests from Latin America by imposing tariffs and limiting quotas. Though controversial, these measures were deemed essential by the European Union, whose members argued that their abolition would lead to the collapse of small farming complexes across the ACP at the hands of the ruthlessly efficient American corporate juggernauts.

The European Union's protectionist approach may have been rooted in noble intentions (toward the ACP nations), but it had an adverse knock-on effect on production costs. The policy tantamounted to a subsidy on inefficient farming practices that subdued competition and all but eliminated the need for innovation. The cost structure was also exacerbated by factors such as hilly terrain, sub-par soil, hurricanes, high wage structures, and high shipping costs. Most of these hurdles were absent in Ecuador, Colombia, and the other Latin countries where Chiquita and Dole had their plantations. As a result, the cost of a harvest in an ACP nation could soar past the $500 per ton mark, while that at a Latin American plantation averaged closer to just $160 per ton.

Chiquita and Dole—formerly the United Fruit Company and Standard Fruit Company, respectively—had over the decades reinvented themselves as modern corporations. They had successfully shed their reputations as the motors powering capitalist imperialism in Latin America on behalf of the United States. Still, they remained influential in the halls of Washington, D.C.; Chiquita particularly so. In response to the banana regime that was hurting their exports to Europe, they leveraged their political clout to lobby the US government to take up the matter of the banana regime with the WTO—the de facto guardian of free trade and the only international body with a mandate to resolve trade disputes between nations. In 1996, Chiquita CEO Carl Lindner Jr. reportedly financed campaigns on both sides of the political aisle and went as far as flying former Senate Majority Leader Bob Dole (no relationship to Dole Fruit Company) during his presidential campaign, using jets affiliated with the Lindner family's corporate interests. In May of 1996, the lobbying culminated in the United States filing a complaint at the WTO. The objection was coordinated with other similar complaints filed in quick succession by Ecuador, Honduras, Guatemala, and Mexico. Within 24 hours, Lindner donated $500,000 to the Democratic Party. It was a gesture rooted in the principle of reciprocation and one that hinted at the real dynamo behind the filings.

The complaints against the European Union were central to the ethos of free trade championed by the WTO. They argued that the removal of dependencies would promote a higher quality product and a lower cost structure, both of which would benefit the European taxpayer footing the bill of subsidies. This, of course, came at the risk of ruin for the ACP growers, furthering the divide between rich and poor. It was clear for all to see that what was at stake was a battle of ideals that transcended trade—a tug of war pitting Old World protectionism against New World liberalism.

The following year, the WTO panel handling the complaints delivered its ruling in favor of the United States. It found the European Union to be in violation of free trade rules on 16 counts, the most prominent of which was *"the EU's assignment of import licenses for Latin American bananas to French and British companies, which took away a major part of the banana distribution business US companies had developed over this century."* But although the fragile WTO had the jurisdiction to make the ruling, it lacked the teeth to enforce compliance. It did not come as a surprise, then, that 24 months after the ruling, the changes made to the existing European banana regime remained largely cosmetic.

The persistence of the banana regime nibbled away at the patience of those championing the American *dollar banana*, and ultimately drove them to retaliate by lobbying for punitive trade tariffs on general European imports to the United States. The sanctions would be broad in scope, impacting items ranging from candles and cashmeres to wafers and waffles. The resultant damage to European businesses was estimated at $250 million, drawing the ire of the European Union, but also dragging them back to the negotiating table.

In 1999, the Europeans finally relented and agreed to take practical steps to level the playing field for the American fruit corporations. A new banana regime was drawn up, under which substantial European import licenses—quotas, essentially— would be issued to Chiquita and Dole starting in January of 2006. (The seven-year respite was designed to provide the ACP nations with sufficient time to mitigate the impact of the transition on their harvest.)

But first, there was an important intermediary milestone that had to be met by July 2001, one concerning a system for distributing the new quotas among the American corporates. Chiquita and Dole—having won the Banana Wars and earned a protectionist right to supply Europe with their Latin-American grown bananas—now found themselves locking horns over how the import licenses would be divided amongst themselves. The split would ultimately dictate each party's share of the European market starting in 2006.

Two license distribution mechanisms were proposed to resolve the matter. The first, advocated by Chiquita, pushed for a system founded on past performance. Under the scheme, quotas would be awarded to importers based on their respective market shares during the period immediately following the establishment of the old banana regime. That corresponded to the period 1994-96, during which Chiquita led Dole in the market.

The second mechanism, championed by Dole, favored a first-come, first-served system that rewarded growers on their present supply capacity at a time when Dole was now leading Chiquita thanks to smart investments in Latin America as well as in some ACP nations.

Historically, Dole had been more accommodating to the policies of the European Union. This expounded its sense of entitlement to a quota distribution mechanism that favored it over Chiquita. To match this ambition, Dole had gambled on growing its capacity, and now found itself burdened with an excess of supply. It was a calculated move, made in the hope that the first-come, first-served quota system would materialize and grant it the lion's share of quotas to the lucrative European markets.

Adversity and opportunity make for an odd couple. Yet, one seldom makes an appearance without the other. In the backdrop of these events, our motley crew of fruit distributors—scattered along the length of the Silk Road and spearheaded by Nahas—created enough legroom for ourselves to capitalize on events. This was true even though our markets lay outside the borders of the European Union—the geography central to the Banana Wars. During the critical period between the agreement on the new banana regime in 1999 and the adoption of the quota-distribution mechanism in 2001, we would maneuver to capitalize on the dogfight playing out between Chiquita and Dole.

Our primary objective was to expand our distribution operation to scope every former Soviet state that met the simple prerequisite of a foreign currency exchange market. The ability to buy and transfer dollars out of a country after a sale enabled us to pay our suppliers and to cash in our profits. But even then, our expansion drive faced one major obstacle: securing a reliable supply of bananas. While we did have a strong relationship with Dole in Turkey, a longstanding policy upheld by the company limited the scope of their partnerships with each distributor to just one market. Until Nahas came along, that is. For him, they made an exception.

Thus, Dole, on a mad-dash grab for new dumping grounds to absorb its excess supply, found sanctuary in our group. As production capacity was ramped up in Ecuador, Colombia and elsewhere, we provided Dole with one outlet after another to unload their bananas—first in markets surrounding the Black Sea, and then in the vicinity of the Caspian Sea. The footprint of our distribution network expanded to encompass Romania, Moldova, Georgia, Armenia, Azerbaijan, Kazakhstan, and Kyrgyzstan. In each of those countries, we would become the first to import the Cavendish banana—as we had done in Turkey earlier—reinforcing our reputation as pioneers. Where our intention was to profit on distribution from every sale, Dole's motive was to gain a favorable share of the EU's import license quotas in the eventuality that the first-come, first-served system were to be adopted. The company set its eyes on the bigger prizes in Germany, France, and the UK, but it required our markets to offload the surplus capacity it was building in the interim.

In July of 2001, word was out that the license-distribution decision would favor Dole's first-come, first-served system. It was only reasonable that quotas were granted based on current, rather than historical, capabilities. The ruling would be a victory not just for Dole, but for us distributors as well: it meant that we would secure Dole's generous supply volumes until at least 2006 as the company sought to maintain its high production capacity in preparation for the European market.

But it was not to be.

For even as Dole was investing to grow its capacity, Chiquita was channeling funds toward supporting political campaigns. Lindner, whom the Clintons hosted at the White House's Lincoln Bedroom overnight, managed to secure a last-minute reversal of the decision through a relentless lobbying drive. A system based on historical performance, favoring Chiquita, was announced the very next day.

Dole complained, arguing the ruling was contrary to the principles of free trade and would lead to supply disruptions. Chiquita was still not entirely satisfied. Emboldened by the victory, it was now protesting (to no avail) that the accord failed to address $200 million in compensation for losses it incurred because of the old regime.

CHAPTER FIVE
TURKISH PROTECTIONISM: PUTTING THE BAN IN BANANAS

After the Banana Wars, the second geopolitical challenge we contended with was the increasingly protectionist line taken by the Turkish government toward the importation of bananas.

In early 2003, a technical paper was published by professors of the Department of Agricultural Economics at Süleyman Demirel University in Isparta, Turkey, in collaboration with Ohio State University. The research, titled "Measuring the Market Power of the Banana Import Market in Turkey," made for a peculiar topic. Its scope was indeed too narrow to have arisen outside of any context.

My immediate thoughts upon learning of the research veered toward suspicion. Every reaction is born of an action, and I doubted that this paper was defying any Newtonian laws. Having a major stake in Turkey's banana market, I considered the matter worth a closer look. Perhaps someone somewhere had an agenda, and they were piggybacking on the credibility of academic circles to push that agenda.

The stated intention of the publication was to prove or disprove the theory that the power carried by multinational corporations in the global banana trade "suggested the presence of underlying structural forces that could facilitate price-enhancing market power [in Turkey]." Using data from 1984-2000, the authors employed a model for deriving the degree of market power held by banana importers. The model concluded that importers wielded a Market Power Parameter of 0.19. Expressed qualitatively, this indicated that "the banana import market in Turkey is not perfectly competitive, but the behavior of firms is much closer to price-taking than to collusion."

It was a delicately worded finding. On one hand, it suggested banana importers like us were guilty of collusion—though *not quite* so. On the other, it trumpeted a victory for the conservative voices inside Turkey's government as the force that—through its protectionist policies—kept the moral compass of importers from tilting deeper into "guilty" territory. By imposing astronomical import taxes to protect domestic producers, the Ministry of Agriculture and Rural Affairs (MARA) had triumphed in its mandated quest to curtail oligopolistic behavior.

MARA had earlier pushed for increased import restrictions to protect local farmers. This, however, backfired as it resulted in the doubling of the price of bananas for the consumer. It was an especially troubling situation because the banana is an essential food staple and, as the paper correctly asserts, local banana production sufficed to satiate just 30 percent of Turkey's enormous appetite—which had worked up to 188,000 tons in 2000. As a result, an embattled MARA was now under scrutiny for its protectionist practices, which were contrary to the principles of free trade upheld by Turkey since joining the WTO. The research, however, with bold claims referencing government action as the driver behind the weakened market power of multinational corporates in Turkey, appeared to justify MARA's policies.

In fact, the serendipitous timing of the paper corresponded with MARA's reversal of a complete (though short-lived) ban on banana imports to Turkey after Ecuador filed a complaint with the WTO. The ban had been three years in the making, culminating from a series of unchecked import restrictions. It brought our sales to a screeching halt, and the gains we made with Dole during the Banana Wars were now under serious threat.

As market leaders, we stood to lose the most. Not only did the import restrictions place our operation in Turkey in jeopardy, but they also threatened the other distribution networks we operated across the region that leveraged our volumes in Turkey for supply chain synergies and economies of scale.

Of course, the restrictions also hurt the interests of Dole, Chiquita, and, by extension, the United States. MARA suddenly found itself upsetting the world's superpower to appease the relatively small-scale local banana growers. In doing so, it became increasingly detached from Turkey's broader strategic imperative.

The research paper was, in my opinion, a partisan commissioning aimed at salvaging MARA's reputation. What initially appeared to be a highly peculiar topic was making complete sense when examined in the context of MARA's predicament.

It was in fact Nahas—in his capacity as the Honorary Consul General of Ecuador in Istanbul—who spearheaded the effort to contest MARA's ban by nudging Ecuador to act through the WTO. Our biggest allies would prove to be Ivonne Baki, a long-time friend who was also the Ecuadorian

Ambassador to the United States, and Ecuadorian President Jamil Mahuad. The fact that both Baki and Mahuad are of Lebanese origin made it easier for Nahas to have their ears.

The saga neared its climax on the afternoon of March 15, 2001, when the Sanitary and Phytosanitary (SPS) Committee at the WTO was approaching the penultimate dispute on an agenda that had exhausted the best part of the past two days. Already ticked off the agenda were deliberations concerning several trade disputes raised under the guise of food safety and other animal and plant-related pests and diseases. Following the order of the day, Argentina's grievances toward Venezuela's phytosanitary requirements for garlic and potato imports had been covered. Also checked were Chile's complaints about Bolivian restrictions on imports of poultry items, and Canada's objections to India's ban on—of all things—bovine semen imports. Next up was Ecuador's complaint against Turkey's restrictions on banana imports.

Ecuador's premise, amidst the sudden appearance of a laboratory-testing bottleneck, was that "the Turkish authorities were issuing phytosanitary control certificates for a specific and limited volume of bananas, a volume believed to be small when compared to the tonnage of normal banana shipments." Such measures, Ecuador conveyed, were designed to restrict the entrance of bananas from Ecuador into the Turkish market. Turkey's representative retorted in brief, stating that the restrictions were in fact driven by a limited phytosanitary testing capability. Turkey had only 15 laboratories at its disposal and was otherwise claiming complete conformity to the terms of the SPS treaty.

The issue, still unresolved, would be taken up during the next SPS meeting four months later. Ahead of that second meeting, Nahas and I—working with a team of lawyers—brainstormed a set of 18 fact-finding questions on behalf of Ecuador that would require answers from Turkey. The responses would have to be submitted ahead of the gathering and would provide the foundation for discourse. In truth, the questions were aimed at ramping-up the pressure on MARA. They were designed to unmask the Turkish banana-import ban for what it was: a protectionist policy meant to appease a base of local growers, rather than a response to the advertised phytosanitary testing limitations.

The first and most important of the 18 questions probed the motive of a *Kontrol Belgesi*, the name attached to the Inspection Certificate. Was the *Kontrol Belgesi* an SPS mechanism, an import-monitoring instrument, or a specific trait of a de facto import licensing system?

A related question was designed to show that until the introduction of the import restrictions, the *Kontrol Belgesi* had never been subject to quantity limitations; in practice, certificates had been issued for up to one million cases of bananas at a time, compared with just 10,000 cases now.

In the interim, the restrictions on banana imports still holding, our high-cost structure and the continued disappearance of revenues was leading us to hemorrhage financially. We were hurting bad. Every delay in the resumption of business-as-usual increased the likelihood that all importers would be pulled back to the starting line once the restrictions were eventually lifted, threatening our position as market leaders.

Turkey's response to the 18 questions came on July 10 of 2001, the day of the next SPS meeting. The timing was designed to buy Turkey time; Ecuador's representatives would not be able to draw a counter-response before the meeting, dragging the matter further. Also, the replies were largely superficial and riddled with inconsistencies.

It was a clear stalling tactic. Additionally, we were now experiencing unexplained delays in the issuance of import licenses of up to 1 week—a lifetime in banana years.

Once the second WTO meeting was underway, the European communities—siding with Ecuador—requested Turkey's response to the 18 questions. The interference provided a damaging psychological blow. Turkey, which was at that time jockeying for a star on the EU flag, was made to appear like it was reneging on a commitment to reform its business environment—one of many prerequisites to joining the European Union. Furthermore, Chile and Colombia—restless over how *Kontrol Belgesi* regulations might curtail their own exports to Turkey—were now requesting that they be kept in the loop on all developments. The interest in the matter had suddenly escalated to a level that Turkey was uncomfortable with.

The limitation on banana imports was quickly spilling into a full-fledged public relations disaster. The speed and ferocity with which a complaint was being dealt with at the WTO had caught Turkey flatfooted. But Turkey would not relent, and the ensuing tug-of-war persisted until Ecuador requested the establishment of a WTO panel to challenge Turkey's import procedures for fresh fruit in June of 2002. It was only after this request was accepted by the WTO that the Turkish side finally announced it would revise its procedures, and the dispute was settled. The reversal was a victory for free trade against protectionism.

While it is impossible to claim with outright certainty that free trade provides the nobler path (as compared to protectionism), one thing was certain: Turkey had committed to fair trade when it became a WTO member. The time to walk the talk had arrived. And yet, the hypocrisy of politics the world over reveals that everyone seems to want the best of both worlds and applies each principle only where it serves their own interests. Even the WTO, the supposed guardian of free trade, is often criticized for serving free trade only as far as its funding entities allow it to do so.

The relaxation of restrictions around the *Kontrol Belgesi* was another victory for us, but the damage had already been done. The ban proved to be a great leveler. The cards had been reshuffled and the banana market's main players were now of comparable prominence, having lost their shares of the market to the operational hiatus. For us specifically, being robbed of our market leadership position was a setback from which we would never completely recover. But we would soldier on.

CHAPTER SIX
A REGIONAL BOOM: FROM PIPE DREAM TO PIPELINE

The cross-Atlantic Banana Wars and Turkey's ban on imported bananas presented us with two existential threats rooted in the geopolitics of supply. We emerged from those challenges with varying degrees of success. Critically, we were still standing, and our gaze now turned toward the third and last of the geopolitical themes highlighted aboard the *Hiawatha*: the much-anticipated Baku-Tbilisi-Ceyhan pipeline. Without the pipeline, there was little hope for economic prosperity in the region.

The Caspian Sea hides a treasure trove of black gold: petroleum. By some estimates, the basin sits on combined proven and probable reserves of oil and gas worth 50 billion barrels and 9 trillion cubic meters, respectively. Historically, these fossil fuel deposits lay entrenched deep inside Soviet territory with limited investments in infrastructure to enable their efficient extraction. They had also been at the heart of political and military conflicts that date as far back as the Bolshevik invasion of Azerbaijan in 1920 and the Battle of Stalingrad—one of WWII's deadliest flashpoints—in 1942.

The lifting of the Iron Curtain in 1991 provided a first real opportunity for pumping the riches of the Caspian Sea to world markets. That feat had thus far proven elusive because of one prominent geographical feature of the Caspian Sea: it is landlocked. The solution to this problem lay in the construction of a pipeline linking the Caspian Sea to a port with easy access to international waters. It was both technologically and geologically feasible to do so; the complication lay in routing the pipeline in a manner that satisfied the major political powers at hand. A path linking the Caspian Sea to the Baltic Sea northward passed strictly through Russian territory, which the Americans and Europeans would try to veto. Directing the pipeline southward, toward the Arabian Sea, would require passage not only through Iran, but possibly also Afghanistan and Pakistan—a path that offered insurmountable security challenges.

The only remaining alternative was to roll out the pipeline westward to the Mediterranean Sea. Still, this route would be complicated as it involved traversing multiple countries—namely, Azerbaijan, Turkey and *either* Georgia *or* Armenia (but importantly not both). It would also need to pass muster with major powers further out, primarily the US, Russia, and the European Union. Finally, the pipeline would have to consider the interests of other nations that held sovereignty claims on the Caspian's reserves, primarily Kazakhstan and Turkmenistan. (The Black Sea, another alternative westward, was a non-starter because of the Bosporus chokehold and the devastating environmental impact an oil spill would have on the sea's confined waters.)

With the fall of the Soviet Union, the newly independent Republic of Turkmenistan began selling concessions permitting the excavation of oil and gas in the Caspian Sea. The concessions were granted at exceptionally low prices as there was no feasible way to connect the petroleum with buyers internationally. To buy a concession was to make a bet that had not paid off for the past 100 years. Still, a small number of colorful adventurers took that gamble for as modest a fee as $100,000 a pop.

Fig. 2 Map depicting route of the Baku-Tbilisi-Ceyhan pipeline.

One such player was Roger Tamraz. A self-styled Egyptian venture capitalist born to Lebanese parents, Tamraz acquired concessions from Turkmenistan in two different blocks, reported to hold 1 billion barrels of oil. Without a pipeline, however, he might as well have placed his chips on 1 billion barrels of pie in the sky.

Tamraz proceeded to focus his efforts on assembling a consortium that could build a pipeline to the Mediterranean and liberate the oil. As a pragmatist, he envisioned a pipeline that took the shortest and consequently cheapest route. But that route would pass through two warring countries: Azerbaijan and

Armenia. A prerequisite peace treaty between the two nations was in order.

A canny soul, Tamraz trumpeted his initiative in Washington, D.C. and the region as a peace pipeline. The proposed pipeline would not only serve American interests but would also create American jobs stemming from the supply of raw material and the provision of technical expertise. Such was the line Tamraz brought—along with contributions to the Democratic Party—all the way into several White House functions hosted by President Bill Clinton and Vice President Al Gore.

Crucially, Tamraz's route met two key American geopolitical imperatives. First, it avoided the territories of Russia, Iran, Afghanistan, and Pakistan. Second, it served to decrease reliance on Arab oil, albeit slightly.

The proposed Azeri-Armenian peace treaty would build on the principle of *land for right-of-passage*. Under such a deal, Russian-backed Armenia would return to Azerbaijan the regions of Nagorno-Karabakh and seven smaller territories that it had seized in a conflict dating back to 1988. In return, the pipeline would be directed through Armenia, allowing the country to benefit from associated tariffs and transit fees. Thus, Tamraz established channels for shuttle diplomacy between Azerbaijan and Armenia.

Armenia showed preparedness for only a partial return of the land it had acquired from the Nagorno-Karabakh conflict, but President Ilham Aliev of Azerbaijan made it clear that he would accept nothing short of a full return of land—a demand that upended the negotiations prematurely. Aliev had set his sights on an alternative route that, despite being longer, flowed through Georgia to bypass Armenia. He later famously said that "If we succeed with this project, the Armenians will end in complete isolation, which would create an additional problem for their future, their already bleak future." The statement reflected the sentiment between the two nations at the time, an attitude that threatened to nip Tamraz's initiative in the bud.

As if that were not enough, the proposed pipeline also faced navigating the thorny issue of Turko-Armenian diplomatic relations—all but non-existent at the time.

The final nail in the coffin to Tamraz's pipeline was delivered by a second competing consortium, one consisting of bigger, more powerful oil companies. Headed by BP, the outfit wielded enough power to distance Tamraz from the White House and drag his pipeline proposal under the spotlight of a federal grand jury investigation. The issue? Whether "anyone tried to bribe or pressure Clinton administration officials." For good measure, reports of Tamraz embezzling $200 million in Lebanon—allegations he denies—suddenly surfaced, as did the issue of a Lebanese military court condemning him to 15 years of hard labor for "contacts with the Israeli enemy."

The consortium led by BP triumphed in the end. A final agreement for a Baku-Tbilisi-Ceyhan pipeline was inked in 1999. On Azerbaijan's insistence, the oil would flow via the longer road northward through Georgia, and then south again to bypass Armenia.

The deal was a devastating blow for Armenia. But for everyone else betting on doing business in the region, here was finally the first tangible step from pipe dream to pipeline. Even Tamraz would benefit from the deal, as he had beaten BP to signing the original pipeline right-of-way transit agreement with the government of Turkey. The right-of-way claim would eventually be sold by Tamraz to the BP-led consortium. Additionally, Tamraz could now deliver the bounty of his Turkmenistan concessions to the world.

The Baku-Tbilisi-Ceyhan pipeline stands as an architectural marvel. Costing $3.9 billion, it passes through 1,768 km of hills and rivers. It was built with a capacity to transport 1 million barrels of black gold daily from fields operated by Azerbaijan, Turkmenistan, and Kazakhstan to the world. With the pipeline in place, and the first delivery received in Ceyhan along the Mediterranean Sea in May of 2006, the countries involved took on a greatly improved status among the circles of the political and business elite. (They also incurred increasing animosity from those left out of the equation—primarily Russia, whose wrath would sometimes spill out of hand, as any Georgian surviving the Russo-Georgian war of 2008 would testify.) In just one year, Azerbaijan's GDP grew by a staggering 35 percent; Georgia and Turkey received annual fees of $60 and $200 million, respectively, for transit rights alone. And of course, a whole new world of commerce, industry, and opportunity sprang up along the pipeline's silky route.

That world would need to be fed bananas. And chicken.

No one was better positioned to supply those markets than we were.

And supply we did.

CHAPTER SEVEN
OUR FIRST MOVE: DOLLAR BANANAS

Our venture's first big effort was in bananas. Moving that challenging product taught me many lessons in the dynamics of trade and supply. Gaining an understanding of the unusual nature of the fruit itself was critical to acquiring those lessons.

To start off, bananas have issues. They really do. In addition to the unusually complex geopolitical nature of the global banana trade, the banana as a fruit—or, more precisely, a berry—possesses three encumbering physical traits. First, it is perishable, with a shelf life of just 60 days from the time of harvest. Second, it is sensitive, making it prone to damage during handling. Third, despite its standing as the world's most cultivated fruit crop, it is prone to disease and remains on the cusp of commercial extinction. Of course, I am talking about the Grand Nain variety—the name itself an oxymoron, translating from French to Large Dwarf—popularized as the Chiquita Banana. The Grand Nain, a Cavendish cultivar, today accounts for very nearly 100 percent of all internationally traded bananas.

These issues are prominent in the Grand Nain, despite it being the cream of the crop of the banana world. While there exist a thousand other candidate cultivars (a keen-eyed jungle trekker is bound to come across as many banana varieties as wild orchids), none are known to offer the qualities required for cash-crop grade domestication. Consumers look for nutritional value, taste, and texture—including the absence of seeds. *Bananeros* seek all that, and then some. A workable variety needs to impress with a large fruit yield, capable of satiating an annual global appetite of over 100 million tons. It needs a pseudo-stem capable of withstanding windthrow, and the harvested fruit must be robust enough to still appear appetizing after it has endured being stacked, handled, and shipped halfway across the world.

But despite its widespread popularity, the Grand Nain banana is far from ideal, because it sits at the very threshold of what is considered workable levels of perishability and robustness. There is absolutely no margin for error. Poor handling, shipping delays, and even oversupply can all lead to heavy financial losses. No one wants to buy bruised bananas, and no one wants to buy black bananas.

I discovered firsthand that trading in a product that is at once perishable, fragile, and existentially threatened has serious implications on two fronts. First, it tests the soundness of the organization's processes and infrastructure to the very limit. In fact, the strain applied on supply chain operations is such that only a select group of organizations ever excel in the world of bananas, be they in production or distribution. Second, it triggers the onset of one variety of physiological stress distinguished by the grinding of the teeth and the occurrence of peptic ulcers.

A far better banana than the Grand Nain is (or perhaps commercially speaking, was) the Big Mike. It was richer and sweeter and sported a thick protective skin. It was also harvested in dense bunches, which made it the darling of the fruit logistics world. In fact, the Big Mike's superiority was such that until the 1950s, it was the main banana cultivar favored across plantations by the corporations. In that era, a grocery store was exponentially more likely to carry Big Mike than the banana with which we are all familiar today. Thus, our Grand Nain took a back seat for 50 full years.

Over that time, a menace was lurking in the fields: Panama Disease. This plant pathogenic fungus would eventually devastate Big Mike plantations the world over, forcing the large corporations to finally transition to the Grand Nain cultivar.

What makes Panama Disease—or any pathogen, for that matter—particularly devastating to commercially grown bananas is the absolute absence of a gene pool. Every Big Mike banana—as with the Grand Nain—is genetically identical to the next, and every banana shoot is an extension of the same herb. A more fitting name might perhaps have been Big Eve, owing to the world's entire pool of Big Mikes descending from a single *mother* specimen.

When one decedent of Eve falls sick because she cannot resist a certain pathogen, the entire collective risks collapse. This is because cultivated bananas propagate through cloning and asexual vegetative reproduction. When a basal shoot of a stem is planted, it carries with it the disease, proliferating the fungus across plantations. Because the shoots carry the same genome, they also bear the same set of failed defenses. Also, the resulting absence of a gene pool makes it highly improbable that an offshoot develops mutations favorable to disease resistance. When Big Mike fell sick, Grand Nain was luckily found to be resistant to the culprit—the Race 1 thread of Panama Disease—and could be used as a substitute cultivar.

But the Grand Nain, too, lacks a gene pool and is currently facing an existential crisis of its own. As of 2021, the cultivar is threatened on two fronts: a fast-spreading Race 4 thread of Panama Disease, and the ominous-sounding Black Sigatoka, another fungus that drastically affects yield quantity and quality. The fungus makes the soil its home, rendering fields useless for decades. As lab scientists race to develop fungicides to save the Grand Nain, jungle trekkers carry on their hunt for a viable alternative cultivar.

Disease is not the only challenge facing banana growers. They are increasingly having to contend with the cyclical effects of the El Niño climate phenomenon, identified by the onset of a large-scale band of warm sea surface water across the central and east-central equatorial Pacific. The warm waters interact with the atmosphere and result in as much as a 35 percent decline in seasonal rainfall. The increased frequency of the El Niño phenomenon has brought about major disruptions to banana production in South America. It has also resulted in increased costs as growers are forced to invest in mitigation measures at the plantations.

The risks associated with dealing in bananas have always been high, but they were well within the tolerance levels we accepted as industry players. The Grand Nain's volatility, however, was a double-edged sword. On the one hand, it raised the stakes for potential competitors, providing the industry with a natural barrier to entry. On the other, the slightest miscalculation in matching supply to demand could cost us an arm. The analogy often used was *winnings trickle in through an IV drip, while losses are counted by the bucketload.* When you won, you made 5 percent; when you lost, it was absolute. Because bananas are perishable, too much supply meant that the excess went to waste. Too little supply, conversely, meant delivery interruptions for our customers and the prospect of losing them to the competition—an equally unfavorable prospect.

A banana is in many ways a disaster on a deadline. From the moment it is harvested, the race against decay begins. The objective: to make it from farm to kitchen in 60 days. As importers and distributors along the Silk Road, the baton was passed along to us at the ports of the Mediterranean Sea and the Black Sea, by which time 30 days had already been lost to handling and shipping. This, of course, assumes no allowances for delays sailing through the Panama Canal (or the Bosporus), bunkering at the Strait of Gibraltar, or chasing shipping documents. The calls at the ports themselves had to be timed to perfection to ensure we had fresh arrivals right when our stock levels permitted. If all of that went well, it left us with 30 days for inland transits, customs clearance, storage, ripening, and delivering to customers.

At each of our offices, warehouses and ripening facilities—from as far west as where the Timiş and Bega rivers converge in Romania to as far east as the shores of Lake Issyk-Kul in Kyrgyzstan—hung a poster of the fruit world's Holy Writ: the Banana Color Chart.

Interpreted properly, the chart told us where we stood in the race to get bananas out the door before they decayed. The chart coded the fruit by color on a scale of 1 to 7. Code 1 was your all-green banana, hard as a hammer, only seen at the plantations. Code 7, at the other end, was a yellow banana with darkened spots. As the fruit climbed up the scale, its complex starch composition broke down into simpler sugars, turning the banana softer and sweeter.

Under optimal storage conditions, bananas continue to ripen over time, reaching code 7 at the end of their 60-day shelf life. But because code 4 and code 5 bananas are needed for delivery to the market daily, it would be poor practice to let an entire shipment ripen to code 7 all at once. Rather, serving the market necessitates the artificial acceleration of the ripening process for small batches at a time. This is achieved by applying ethylene gas and raising the storage temperature. Each ripening cycle requires 3 days, which means that we were having to operate on a continuously rolling forecast. If there was an oversupply of ripe bananas in the market, that led to an instant price war, because the alternative to selling a code 6 (all yellow) or code 7 (spotted) today was the dumpster tomorrow. Undersupply the market with ripe product and you lose customers, as no supermarket outlet wants to be out of stock on what is a top-three grossing item the world over—not for one minute.

This continuous struggle—matching arrivals at the ports to stocks at the warehouse and then ripening batches of bananas to perfectly fulfill rolling demand forecasts—often inspired an ugly side to the distribution business. Competitors spied on each other's operations, while others allegedly colluded to hike sales prices. Others yet, as we will see, lost all sense of sanity and ethics—resorting to assault, arson, kidnapping, and worse.

In Turkey, our largest market, matching supply with demand was less of a problem as we led the competition by a significant margin. As the market leader, we had the biggest influence on setting the sales price. We could also afford to bring rogue competitors back in line in the eventuality of a price war—short-term, that brought about a lose-lose situation; long term, it was different.

When it came to supplier-customer relations, we struggled only when we allowed the customer to dictate terms. This became apparent to me as early as November 1999, while on a mission to visit our nine distribution centers scattered around the country.

Each of those centers operated as a franchise, running its own storage and ripening facilities, as well as a store at the city's main fruit and vegetable bazaar. The franchises also managed small distribution fleets that we owned or leased. The storage and ripening infrastructure located outside Turkey's major cities was mostly set up using insulated temperature-controlled reefer containers. While the operating expenses per case handled at these containers was higher than those at our modern purpose-built facilities in the major cities, we accepted this as the price of flexibility—the containers could be moved overnight to quickly set up new franchises, and they provided a modular solution for rapidly increasing or decreasing storage capacity at specific locations.

The purpose of my 11-day mission was to make a long list of our ad hoc operating procedures across the board, separate the sane ones from the inefficient ones, then standardize and roll out the best of our practices across the nation—all in the name of efficiency and quality. I started off driving over the Fatih Sultan Mehmet Bridge from the European into the Asian side of Istanbul, and on through the district of Avcılar in Izmit. The city was still reeling from the devastation caused by the earthquake a couple of months earlier, in which 20,000 collapsed buildings still lay stacked like fallen dominoes. The destruction soon gave way to normality again as I rode the ferry at Eskihisar on toward my first stop at Bursa. From there, I took the scenic road past Çanakkale, near the archaeological site at Troy, where today stands a giant statue of the Trojan Horse, and on to my second and more notable stop at the metropolitan city of Izmir. The music of Sixpence None the Richer sounded through my earphones as I approached my third stop in Antalya, a popular tourist destination along the Mediterranean. I then negotiated the meandering roads of the legendary Taurus Mountains on to the

Arabic-speaking part of Turkey for a fourth stop at Mersin. Further stops were made in Kayseri, equally famous for its Seljuk-era city walls and its delicacy pastırma; Gaziantep and Ankara, deep in the heart of Anatolia; and finally, Samsun along the Black Sea. Each of these cities boasted its own flavor of historical and cultural richness, no doubt influenced by the magic of the Silk Road of yore.

A typical day on the tour saw me inspecting the operation at the fruit and vegetable bazaar as early as 4 AM, before heading to our storage and ripening facilities. By noon, I would make a round of our major clients in the area before driving off to spend the evening at the next city. On the next day, the routine started over. At times, I would pass a day experiencing places that were too good to miss out, such as the tree houses built around the Lycian ruins at Olympos, where white cheese and watermelon was the order of the day. Or I would stop to enjoy a Cappadocian sunset with a glass of white wine and strawberries after a day at the Kaymaklı underground city. When I was on the road and at the next franchise, it was back to analyzing processes and collecting data, crunching the numbers, and doing a lot of listening and a lot of learning.

At each of our locations, I looked at a specific set of vital indicators that revealed a divide in the way that we went about our business. At times, the chasm was so vast that it felt like I was visiting different organizations entirely. The contrast was most pronounced when comparing two franchises in particular: one was run by Gypsy Kings devotee Cemal Çifci in Izmir—host to Turkey's third largest population after Istanbul and the capital, Ankara; the second, in the sleepy town of Samsun along the Black Sea, managed by gentlemen by the name of Ismail Sakalaki.

The following short extracts from my notes at the time highlight some of our operational inconsistencies across those two locations:

Izmir, 12 November 1999

Average Daily Sales per Unit of Storage (40-ft. container)
14.6 boxes
Average Daily Sales per Employee
46.7 boxes
Ratio of First- to Second- to Third-Quality bananas (last 7 days)
40:40:20

- *Quality of bananas reaching customers is below par and leading us to lose sales to important supermarket chains. Touring supermarkets with Çifci, we saw that product was further deteriorating at their stores because of poor handling. In some instances, bananas are stacked 15 cases high, turning them into milkshakes before they even reached the shelves. In other instances, bananas were stored with other fruits, reducing their shelf life. Changes were agreed to distribution schedules to ensure better quality product on the shelves. Also, Çifci to educate our clients on product handling.*

- *Despite the low Average Daily Sales to Unit of Storage ratio, Çifci is requesting to increase storage capacity by 50% ahead of an expected seasonal sales spike. Çifci to receive cross-training on ripening and storage management.*

- *Storage containers are positioned in two straight open rows. It takes 1 minute 20 seconds for a forklift to drag a pallet from one end of the depot to the other, unnecessarily exposing product to the elements.*

- *Product received aboard the M/V Polar Uruguay shows signs of chilling. Truck temperature reports from Istanbul to Izmir were examined and show bananas were stored at 6 degrees Celsius, and not 13 degrees Celsius. Note to further investigate and file a claim with trucking company.*

- *Bananas are priced up to 10% higher than Del Monte's product. Çifci not worried, asserting, "Our customers are the most loyal in Turkey." Engaging with some clients at the bazaar, my empirical findings are that vast majority of buyers find our bananas overpriced and below par on quality.*

Samsun, 21 November 1999

Average Daily Sales per Unit of Storage (40-ft. container)
32.4 boxes

Average Daily Sales per Employee
68.8 boxes

Ratio of First- to Second- to Third-Quality bananas (last 7 days)
80:15:5

- *Samsun is the most impressive of our operations and can act as a model to be replicated elsewhere. We enjoy 75% market share, and our First-Quality bananas occupy shelves at every major supermarket.*
- *Cold stores are neatly arranged in 4 rows and are provided easy access to loading/unloading docks.*
- *Sakalaki appears to know every move made by the competition.*
- *An agreement is in place with Turkish Post (PTT) to distribute product across Samsun's suburbs.*
- *A refrigerated storage room is under construction at our*

> *store inside Samsun's fruit and vegetable bazaar. Directly facing us sits Orhan Oz, who appears to have switched supplier from Chiquita to Del Monte.*

- *Sakalaki runs a unique sales schedule. Customers are assigned weekly quantities and product pickup slots, giving us increased visibility over sales, and laying the groundwork for our ripening schedule. For example, one customer might be scheduled 100 deliveries on Mondays, Wednesdays, and Fridays. Another customer's schedule might read 10 cases daily. This is having a positive knock-off effect on our Ratio of First- to Second- to Third-Quality bananas.*

Simple as it sounds, this last part—scheduling sales on our timeframe rather than on the buyer's terms—was a novel masterstroke that dramatically improved the accuracy of our rolling forecast. It subsequently enabled us to perfect our ripening schedules vis-à-vis daily demand. Additionally, it allowed for improved quality—with less carryover decaying stocks—and increased customer loyalty.

It also helped that the person managing the franchise on location, Sakalaki, was a true *bananero* who understood the intricacies of the ripening process. For instance, he knew how the stacking formation of banana cases or the timing of controlled temperature fluctuations affected the taste, texture, and appearance of the fruit. The superior quality we achieved in Samsun—but lacked in Izmir— was what won us market share there, and in turn gave us control of delivery schedules to our clients. As a seasoned marketeer, Sakalaki had mastered all of this. Furthermore, he recognized that dipping a thick moustache into the local beverage of choice—tea enjoyed in a Turkish tea glass with two sugar cubes—sold more bananas to a fruit peddler than a solitary caramel macchiato knocked back behind the wheel on the drive to work.

Sakalaki's approach provided the basis for a model that we would soon strive to roll out across all of our locations.

CHAPTER EIGHT
OUR NEXT MOVE:
THE TYSON LEG-QUARTER
AND THE SADIA GRILLER

I vividly remember the first time I heard the name Samir Sidani. I was barely approaching my teen years, and he, despite being my first cousin, was breaking 45. Hanging around my grandmother's divan at the Manara district in Beirut, I overheard my uncle and aunt reciting his conquests. The stories were traded with such zeal and glorified pride that there was no telling if or where the conversation veered out of the domain of established fact and into the realm of the apocryphal.

"He was the first entrepreneur to export as much as a chicken *feather* to Russia," my uncle started.

"I know," my aunt retorted. "In Russia, he had to repel the Mafia before he could walk away with his cash in a briefcase!" Her overflowing pride was betraying her lack of knowledge of trade finance.

My uncle, not to be outdone, was now doubling down with names and numbers to lend credence to his own rendering of events.

"...and when Red Hudson decided to sell to Don Tyson for $650 million, Samir established Meat Products International on his own. He wasn't happy about missing out on the top exports job after the merger, having held that position earlier with Hudson. Still, he went on to beat them to the rest of the Soviet states," he concluded, in a rather celebratory tone. "After all, it was he who helped grow Hudson's fortunes past the billion-dollar mark even before joining them—as their financier at Bank of America."

As a 12-year-old snooping on the conversation, I was enchanted by the mystic nature of Sidani's odyssey in those faraway lands. I wanted in.

But much as Samir Sidani was a household name in my circles growing up, I wouldn't get the chance to put a face to the name until a couple of weeks before setting out for Istanbul, eight years later. His persona, I discovered, was distinguished by charismatic flair and sharp business acumen. A towering physique hinted to his former life as an athlete and indeed Lebanese basketball champion. Naturally, his beverage of choice was hard *whisky*—spelled the Scottish way to emphasize oomph. Despite, or perhaps because of these superhero qualities, the Miniature Yorkshire Terrier was his dog breed of preference, which I thought largely spoke for an unquenchable thirst for affection.

Context for Sidani's story begins in 1997, when Hudson Foods—America's fourth largest poultry meat processor—was ensnared in a debacle following the sale of ground beef contaminated with E. coli. The company was forced to recall 11 thousand tons of meat from the market, one of the largest recalls on record. Hudson Foods itself, along with two employees, would later be indicted on federal charges for providing a misleading account on the condition of the product. The fallout proved irreparably devastating for the brand, leading to a successful takeover bid by Tyson Foods for a discounted price of $640 million.

This is the point at which Sidani's legend emerges. He had earlier left Tyson for Hudson. Now, rather than go back to Tyson on their terms, he broke away and set up Meat Products International, Inc. (MPII), in Rogers, AR—where both Hudson Foods and Tyson Foods are headquartered. At Tyson, Sidani had helped setup the Moscow rep office. It was in moving chicken from the US to Russia that he first made his name in the industry. Years later, we would join forces in expanding that effort across the markets in which we operated our banana cold chains.

The case for exporting American poultry halfway across the world to Russia was first made at the end of the Cold War, when chicken leg-quarters were pushed by the Bush administration to a fragile Soviet Union under the banner of foreign aid. It was distributed through the United States Agency for International Development, commonly known as USAID. The exports were part of a broader effort in support of Mikhail Gorbachev and, later, Boris Yeltsin, both of whom American strategists viewed as liberals driving the transformation of Russia's socialist landscape into a capitalist open market economy. As it turned out, these chicken leg-quarters— they would come to be known as *Nozhki Busha*, or Bush Legs—were something of a double-edged sword for the Russian economy. On the one hand, they provided access to cheap protein. On the other, they further strained an already exhausted collective farming system. Ultimately, the collapse of the Soviet Union in 1991 proved to be the last straw for Russian feed and poultry producers, as the end of state subsidies and a privatization drive led to a 40 percent decline in production capacity for the period ending in 1995.

The widening protein supply deficit in Russia would no longer be plugged by USAID, but by corporations that were now free to operate in a fledgling open economy. Leading the way on the ground was Sidani. In 1991, when helping set up Tysons' Moscow office, he fostered a working relationship with Soyuzcontract, an importer established by two young dynamic Russian entrepreneurs, Mikhail Lubovich and Alexei Goldstein. Over the next six years, Soyuzcontract would grow from practically nothing into a $1 billion business. Although the company would later diversify its interests, it owed its growth to the chicken leg-quarter market that was now touching $500 million in annual sales.

The year 1996 was as big as they came as far as world politics go. Bill Clinton and Boris Yeltsin were both running for reelection as president of the United States and the recently reborn state of Russia, respectively. Ironically, the two Cold War adversaries were rooting for each other. Clinton was openly promoting Yeltsin as a progressive reformist who would be a worthy opponent to the cunning communist antagonist, Gennadi Zyuganov. Yeltsin, on the other hand, was cheering on Clinton for championing the approval of a proposed $10.2 billion IMF loan to support modernizing the Russian economy.

And just in case, Yeltsin was taking out insurance on Clinton's support. He threatened to ban the import of American chicken to Russia—on sanitary grounds. The move would prove to be a vintage political maneuver, straight from the Russian playbook. Chicken protein represented close to a third of American exports to Russia, and by building hype around a prospective ban, Yeltsin was dealing Clinton a bleak hand at a time critically close to the elections.

Crucially, Yeltsin understood that for Clinton, poultry was personal. Clinton was previously Governor of Arkansas, where Tyson Foods—the world's largest chicken processing company—was slaughtering 3.5 million birds a day and supplying close to 40 percent of all poultry exports to Russia. Arkansas naturally represented the state where Clinton drew the core of his grassroots support. Don Tyson, at the helm of Tyson Foods and running an organization with a budget reportedly double that of Arkansas, traditionally threw the full weight of his political clout behind Clinton. Over the years, he had funneled thousands of dollars toward campaign donations and even provided Clinton with private jet travel on multiple occasions. Tyson and the other heads of Arkansas' poultry producing families—collectively known as the Chicken Kings—often congregated at The Poultry Federation's headquarters in Little Rock, colloquially known as The Chicken House. From there, they ran a lobby with formidable leverage over the voices and wallets of hundreds of thousands of voters. Clinton was wary that disappointing the Chicken Kings on the Russian file would not bode well for him in the elections.

Yeltsin's gambit played out rapidly and decisively. Things boiled to a climax at the optimistically named "Summit of Peacemakers," hosted by Egyptian President Hosni Mubarak at the Red Sea resort of Sharm el-Sheikh in March of 1996. With 30 world leaders present and an agenda brimming with retro '90s parlance of an "Israeli-Palestinian peace process" and "NATO's Bosnia deployment," it came as little surprise to the peacemakers that the most hyped outcome of the summit was a seemingly *quid pro quo* exchange between Clinton and Yeltsin, captured in a memo leaked to the media. The memo paraphrases Clinton, protesting the Russian poultry ban: "This is a big issue, especially since about 40 percent of US poultry is produced in Arkansas. An effort should be made to keep such things from getting out of hand." Yeltsin obliged by responding that "A leader of international stature such as President Clinton should support Russia, and that means supporting Boris Yeltsin. Thought should be given to how to do that wisely." A few weeks later, in Moscow, Yeltsin amped up the pressure by telling visiting US Secretary of State Warren Christopher, "Presidents don't do chicken legs," before quipping "If, however, they were women's legs..."

Almost immediately after the spring summit, in time for consolidating the support of the American poultry federation and the Russian populace ahead of the looming election season, the outcome of the leaked exchange materialized. Yeltsin succeeded in his bid for a bumper IMF loan—despite failing to fully comply with the stated preconditions—and American chicken was back on the menu across Russia's kitchens. The cherry on the cake was the opening of several other former Soviet states to business, all of which were still governed by Soviet-era strongmen close to the Russian regime.

This new situation presented Sidani, and ultimately us, with an entryway to supply leg-quarters to the region through ports along the Black Sea.

But what is all this fuss about American exports of chicken leg-quarters? Why not breasts or wings, or maybe whole chickens? The casual observer would have you believe it has to do with meat color preferences varying across the divide, with Americans favoring the white meat of the breast and Russians predisposed to consuming the darker blue meat found in the thigh and drumstick. Truth be told, it is more a matter of ornithology, lifestyle trends, slaughterhouse technology, and economics—in that order.

One of the peculiarities of poultry production is a limitation on output specifications, owing to a bird's anatomy. For what's in a bird? Broadly speaking, to produce one chicken is to produce one breast, one back, one neck, two wings, and two legs. It therefore follows that fulfilling an order for, say, 10,000 chicken breasts will unavoidably yield 10,000 backs, 10,000 necks, 20,000 wings, and 20,000 legs' worth of byproduct. Some of those cuts, of course, are readily marketable, but there is always bound to be more demand for one part over another, making for very tricky production scheduling.

In the US, breasts are indeed the most in-demand, in large part driven by the processed food industry's strong affinity for boneless chicken meat as a raw material. To cope with demand, slaughterhouses are automated. However, the technology allows only for the efficient mechanical deboning—with a quick swoosh of a blade—of the chicken breast. The same cannot be said about other parts. For instance, the meat around the drumstick is held by two bones (the tibia and the fibula) arranged at an awkward angle, rendering it impossible for a mechanical blade to debone robotically. Deboning legs by hand would be so expensive, as it was explained to me at one Atlanta slaughterhouse, that it would be cheaper to dump the parts for pet food. Similarly, the process of deboning wings, backs, and necks is exacerbated by even more complex skeletal structures and lower meat content, making the practice prohibitively expensive even when scaled. Because a disproportionately large chunk of American orders was for chicken breasts, the poultry industry was in a pickle when it came to selling the rest of the chicken parts. Put another way, very few of us visit the grocery store to procure chicken backs.

Luckily, every once in a while—well within the confines of the laws of nature—a freak sociopolitical mutation transpires, manifesting its phenotype in demand patterns for this part or that part of the chicken and providing an unexpected boon for the poultry industry. One such serendipitous event traces its roots back to the winter of 1964, when one Dominic Bellissimo was enjoying his favorite beverage amongst friends at the Anchor Bar joint run by his family. With the clock approaching midnight and his body yearning for a renewed influx of food to counter his rising alcohol content, Dominic asked his mother, Teressa, to cook up something quick for the boys. That request would set the stage for a moment that would drive the Bellissimos into culinary folklore. With the kitchen approaching closure and low on supplies, she grabbed a case of chicken wings that had been accidently delivered by a supplier. Flanked with celery and blue cheese, a maiden version of an essential dish was served. Today, this chicken wings appetizer carries the name of the New York town where the Anchor Bar is still located: *Buffalo*.

By the 1980s, Buffalo wings were in the mainstream in bars across America, and poultry processers could now profitably sell the wings for uses other than just soup stock and petfood. Two decades later, at the turn of the millennium, one could order the snack the world over by its name, Buffalo wings, and expect it to be served the same way. Except in Buffalo, of course, where locals can get away with just *wings*.

Other fortuitous events for the industry included China joining the World Trade Organization in 2001, which created demand for chicken feet literally overnight. For us, the all-important breakthrough was the opening of the Soviet markets, which secured outlets for the cheap chicken leg-quarters rejected by American society and American food processors alike.

The backs had remained a problem until a production tweak allowed line workers to separate the leg from the back at a point higher up from the ground, essentially modifying what was otherwise sold as a whole-leg (thigh and drumstick). This created a means to stowaway substantial portions of the boney back to market as they remained attached to the legs. Thus, with an altered knife-swing pattern, the chicken leg-quarter was born. (The aspiring entrepreneur is hereby invited to try a hand at unlocking a market for the last of the unwanted chicken parts: *necks*.)

American chicken leg-quarters would go on to become the mainstay of American chicken protein exports. It was a product that competed by virtue of its low price. Meanwhile, Brazil—another behemoth of the poultry producing world—turned its attention to high-end whole chicken, a product that sought to differentiate itself on superior quality and branding. Where Tyson was the darling of the leg-quarter world, Brazilian producer Sadia established itself as the benchmark when it came to whole chicken broilers and grillers. As such, the two products—cheap staple leg-quarters and expensive designer whole chicken—competed against each other only as a Zara strappy stretch top rivaled a Chanel tweed jacket. For us, that meant there was room—and indeed opportunity—to consolidate the two under one house.

Of the markets in which we operated, poultry sales were highest in the countries of the Caucasus, a region that takes its name from the transverse mountain system crammed between the Black Sea and the Caspian Sea. The Caucasus comprises a trio of independent states— Georgia, Armenia, and Azerbaijan (in addition to the then troubled Russian republics of Chechnya and Dagestan)—that had been part of the Soviet Union and were now reforming into capitalistic systems.

When those first opened their doors to imports, Nahas was the first to arrive with the dollar bananas—in 1996. It was an expansion drive aligned with Dole's engagement strategy for the Banana Wars, but also one that furthered his legacy as a pioneer, which started with the importation of the first foreign bananas to Turkey and Romania earlier that decade.

As it happens, the infrastructure to store and distribute bananas can be easily tweaked to accommodate frozen chickens by simply adapting the chillers to drop storage temperatures to the required -21 degrees Celsius. Sidani, who had built his reputation on exporting American poultry meats to Russia, had already broken off from Tyson. Still, he had the leverage and the charisma to entice them to partner up in the Caucasus. What he lacked was a vehicle for product distribution there. Nahas, on the other hand, had the infrastructure to distribute, but he remained an oblivious outsider to the poultry world—his interests thus far lay almost strictly within the confines of the banana world. Sidani and Nahas complemented each other like Yin and Yang. It did not take long for them to join forces after they were introduced, and our venture took a giant new step. The rest, as they say, is history.

Our early days in chicken were the most profitable, owing to the supernatural phenomenon of first-mover advantage. The yolk-and-red Tyson logo graced every leg-quarter we imported, which served to set the standard in the region for years and years to come. We were buying leg-quarters for as low as $200 per ton—a fraction of the $1000 per ton demanded for whole chicken—and distributing for at least twice the cost of goods. Of course, all involved knew that our uncharacteristically high profit margins would be impossible to sustain because of the nature of laissez-faire markets and the profit-sniffing competition.

Nevertheless, we did our part to keep barriers to entry as daunting as possible and sought to deter any competition by flooding the market with abnormally large quantities of product—enough to keep the entire population of the Caucasus fed three meals of leg-quarters a day for months. Georgia provided the most convenient points of access to the region, through the Black Sea ports of Poti and Batumi. From there, product was loaded onto trucks and rail wagons and transited to the capital Tbilisi, as well as to neighboring Azerbaijan and Armenia. The same ports would later serve our other destinations in Central Asia further east.

It was a gold rush in the true sense of the word, and no gold rush goes unnoticed.

Barely three months into the venture, the competition had arrived and was already showing signs of the foul play endemic to most Soviet states in the '90s. We became the target of a harassment campaign almost immediately, which went as far as detaining a member of our staff in Georgia for the dubious allegation of an "intention to smuggle bananas".

By the end of 1999, the initial market frenzy had settled. Making money now required a skillset totally different from that required for bulldozing one's way into a market. Henceforth, the name of the game would be an efficient and well-oiled distribution network that competed on traditional corporate tenets. It was out with the muscle, product dumping, and opportunistic spot deals, and in with efficiencies, optimization, and corporate organization.

Under these new slogans, it was no longer acceptable, nor financially viable, to turn a blind eye to the odd missing pallet or the expired lot that went unnoticed deep in the dark Soviet-era cold stores that we operated. We were losing up to 10 percent of our cargo to disorganization, and we figured the bulk of that was happening at the port of Poti. This was also a time in which Tyson was beginning to lose its appetite toward the region—seeing that the end of the gold rush was near, and that harassment and racketeering was on the upswing.

Sidani, to ensure we sustained our source of supply, turned architect for another joint venture, this time with America's largest poultry protein trader at the time: AJC Foods. With our markets getting more and more competitive, the strategy was now to shop around for the cheapest leg-quarters through these traders, rather than stick with a single grower—as was the case with Tyson Foods. One day AJC would supply us with product sourced from Tyson Foods, the next from Wayne Farms, and on yet another from Perdue. So long as it was leg-quarters in the case, AJC brought it and we distributed it.

But our belief was also that competing on cost alone would not be sustainable. There was bound to be a competitor priced cheaper this month or that. Since frozen leg-quarters were a commodity, whose price fluctuated with the prices of their raw material (soy and corn), and since they could technically be stored at the right temperatures for upward of a year, we were always up against the speculative buyer who rested on their stocks until that day came, and they would break us (a near impossible feat in the banana world, owing to the fruit's perishable quality).

No, chicken leg-quarters would not be a sustainable source of profit for long. We would continue dealing in them to maintain a varied offering and to generate sufficient sales volumes that covered a chunk of our overhead costs. But, we believed, the future for prospering in these fledgling economies—on the cusp of an economic windfall from the imminent Baku-Tbilisi-Ceyhan pipeline—lay in building and operating a brand for the real deal: whole chicken broilers, grillers, and Further Processed Products (FPPs)—chicken nuggets, breaded breast fillets and other delectable creations molded from the fleshy part of the bird.

In our view, the gold standard for those products was set by Brazilian producers. The high quality of Brazilian chicken meat was attributable to several factors: the remote locations of the farms (away from polluted population centers), premium feed, clean water, and meticulous attention to quality standards. And if Brazilian chicken was the gold standard, Sadia, the leading brand in that land, was at the top of the chicken world. Leveraging our profile as Dole and Tyson partners across the region, we readied ourselves to knock on their door, equipped with an ego only rivaled by their own.

The person we would have to convince at Sadia was Dr. Natale Motta, a respected industry old-timer from Milan. Dr. Motta was a man of many idiosyncrasies, among which was a superstition to avoid a flight if he was not assigned the 1A seat, and a penchant for settling his lunch and dinner bills—no matter how small—with crisp 500-euro banknotes. He was fluent in five languages and would often start a sentence in one language and conclude it in another. With an illustrious history stretching back to the 1970s, Dr. Motta was the architect behind the largest of Sadia's conquests abroad, including those of the Kuwaiti and Saudi poultry protein markets. Each of those successes added a feather in his cap, amassing him enormous influence at Sadia. His early ventures provided a blueprint that Sadia sought to replicate around the world. In many ways, Dr. Motta was to Sadia and Brazilian poultry exports what Sidani was to Tyson Foods and American poultry exports. Now, he was sensing opportunity in the Caucasus and Turkey, just as we were. Only we were already there, and he was not.

Or, rather, he was halfway there.

Dr. Motta had just completed a tour of the region and was in advanced talks to enter a partnership with one of our smaller competitors. When we reached out to him, his mind had already been made up. As someone who was specialized in building markets from scratch, it came to him as a mere detail that our distribution network was much larger in scale, and his prospective suitor was the underdog. Despite our advances, he would not budge. We were being rejected—something we had not been used to. We were outsiders in Brazil, with nobody to tap for influence or to vouch for us. (Sidani's connections were limited to American suppliers.)

Dr. Motta's talks with our competitor were at such an advanced stage, in fact, that he happened to be in Istanbul for putting the finishing touches to the deal. He was then scheduled to head to Antalya with his wife to enjoy the Mediterranean waters and sun—ingredients for his trademark tan and slicked-back silvery hair.

We were back at the drawing board in our Istanbul office, turning our gaze elsewhere in Brazil. We had begun charting a course to approach Perdigão and Frangosul, who were Brazil's second and third largest providers after Sadia. Despite lacking the exposure and brand awareness that Dr. Motta had built for Sadia outside Brazil, the two producers could supply product of a comparable quality. Before accepting our fate definitively, however, we decided to give Dr. Motta one last call; after all, he was right here in Turkey.

At first, the result was the same: firm rejection. But then, barely 30 minutes after our conversation, he called back. He sounded shaken and spoke with a quavering voice.

"Help, please, we just had a terrible accident," he said. He had been driving his rental to Antalya when they crashed. Since we had just spoken with him, our office number headed the call log on his Nokia Communicator—tempting him to reach out to us before he did anyone else.

"Where are you?"

"I don't know."

"Is everyone all right?"

"My wife is hurt," he said, sounding traumatized. He had good reason to feel so—the accident had resulted in Mrs. Motta suffering several broken bones and the outcome could have easily been worse.

They had driven southward well beyond Izmir, and it would be a three-to-four-hour drive to the nearest major hospital, and twice as far to get to Istanbul.

On learning of the location of the crash, Nahas, in his inimitable fashion, stepped in. He reassured Dr. Motta that he would send an air ambulance to evacuate him and his wife to a hospital and set to work contacting a charterer we often used to book small jets where complicated travel itineraries and remote destinations were involved. Dr. Motta knew that Nahas was under no obligation—humanitarian or otherwise—to go beyond calling the emergency services for a land ambulance. He also realized that by chartering the jet, Nahas was personally incurring a considerable cost. Living through a dark and bloody moment on a distant highway, Dr. Motta would recognize the gesture for what it was: gallant and stately. It was worthy of his lifelong trust, loyalty, and friendship.

Then and there, before the emergency medical responders had even arrived at the scene of the accident, Dr. Motta decided that we would after all be Sadia's partners at every market that we operated from Eastern Europe to Central Asia.

These events went to show that while all the talk of value

proposition, strategic prowess, and operational excellence is certainly worth something, its importance pales in comparison with personal relationships—more so at the highest echelons of influence. Luck played a role as well: the timing and location of Dr. Motta's accident provided the unexpected break we needed to forge our relationship with Sadia.

As I got to know Dr. Motta on a personal level over the next few years, the importance of those lessons would be reinforced repeatedly. I came to realize that Dr. Motta saw himself in us. We shared more than just interests in the poultry trade; we shared common values and aspirations, and we had all grown up on olive oil and charred octopus on that stretch of Mediterranean from Trieste to Beirut.

There was also a great deal of wisdom imparted by Dr. Motta at the operational level. Whereby we were trained to start big, moving container-loads of cheap, dispensable leg-quarters each day, Dr. Motta dedicated his life's work toward the slower-but-surer strategy of brand building. Where we sold chicken, Dr. Motta sold Sadia— dominating market after market one bird at a time. This commitment to the long game required patience and stamina. These were qualities we had to learn as a prerequisite to succeeding in our joint venture with Sadia. And we learned them from Dr. Motta.

CHAPTER NINE
CHAPECÓ SLAUGHTERHOUSE

In November 2000, I was attending routine meetings at Sadia's headquarters in São Paolo, Brazil. I had also scheduled a visit to Chapecó, a smaller agricultural town in the southern state of Santa Catarina. The poultry farming cooperatives and supporting infrastructure in Chapecó, predominantly championed by Sadia, generated roughly 80 percent of the town's GDP. My internal flight was scheduled at the odd time of 6:08 AM, and the return at 8:18 PM the following evening. That gave me enough time to tour one of the facilities hosting a slaughterhouse and a processing plant in the area, as well as a couple of the farms where freshly hatched chicks are raised brooder to broiler.

Once boarding was completed aboard the Rio-Sul-operated Embraer EMB 120, a twin-turboprop with a seating capacity of 30, the captain let us know that the flight time would be 1 hour 7 minutes, which got me speculating—to no avail—about the rationale behind the 6:08 take-off time. It was beautiful flying weather, and by the time we hit our cruising altitude of just 24,000 feet, we were already preparing to descend again. The low-altitude nature of the flight made it possible to enjoy stretches of lush rainforests for most of the journey.

Disembarking onto the desolate apron at Chapecó Airport, I was greeted by Rafael Fehlauer, a cheerful young man to whom I took an immediate liking. Fehlauer was assigned to host me for the duration of my stop, a responsibility that entailed organizing a tour of the supply-side infrastructure there. The main purpose of this was to get to the bottom of endemic delivery issues that were on the rise as the operational and geographic scope of our joint venture with Sadia grew in complexity. By acquiring an understanding of how things worked at the source, I would be better prepared to mitigate the issues we faced as distributors further down the supply chain.

"Oi Bom dia, tudo bem?" Fehlauer started.

"Tudo bom. É bom te ver." I returned the greeting, adding that it was a pleasure making his acquaintance.

With that, we were done with the niceties and I had just about exhausted the breadth of my Portuguese lexicon. It was clear to the both of us that any ensuing conversation that day would remain rather limited in depth.

Fehlauer was in his mid-twenties and full of life. It was not until late that afternoon, over a discussion around the state of Brazilian football and the humiliation of the national team at the World Cup final a couple of years earlier, that I would learn of his complicated relationship with Caipirinhas—a cachaça spirit-and-lime concoction infused with *two full teaspoons of* sugar, which was two more than any purist could tolerate.

As our conversation evolved, it dawned on me that he consumed the beverage not for its molecular alchemy or the nasal notes it exuded, but rather out of remorse. The caipirinha is the national drink of Brazil, and every serving Fehlauer was belting down was transubstantiated into a step down the long road to salvation. It was his way of telling the world he was patriotic again, having earlier denounced the Brazilian squad in a blind fit of rage after Brazil was handed *that* three-nil drubbing by the French. Satisfied I had vindicated Fehlauer on account of the sugar packed Caipirinhas in that way, I spared him the character assassination.

At the slaughterhouse, I was stepping out of the shower and into a pair of white abattoir overalls. I was also provided with special purpose impermeable boots, ear plugs, gloves, and goggles—all equipment designed to minimize the risk of bacterial contamination to the meat. Fehlauer proceeded to lead me to a room with dim red lighting, fittingly known as the "dark room", for the start of our tour.

There was a certain eeriness to the dark room that spoke of a calm before the storm. The ambiance was designed to relax the incoming birds, that were expected to—like most animals—quickly settle when they could no longer discern their surroundings. Little did they know that what was to follow would be anything but settling.

We did not have to wait long for the first batch of birds to arrive. A truck was backing up, loaded with chickens whose short lives—adding up to 21 days inside the egg and another 42 days outside of it—were literally coming to the end of the line. Awaiting them was the dark room, where Fehlauer and I lurked. Ominously for the birds, a team of chicken catchers appeared out of the woodwork and was now lunging at them—grabbing 8 or 10 at a time—and hanging them by the legs on shackles suspended from an overhead rail. The chicken catchers made it look easy.

A few minutes into the routine, Fehlauer directed my gaze toward the source of the red hue in an otherwise perfectly dark room.

"*Tu sabes para que serve isso?*" he asked, testing my knowledge on the purpose of the dimmer, before offering a response in the same breath. "*É para manter as galinhas calmas.*"

"A calm chicken is a happy chicken," I acknowledged, offering a barely visible thumbs-up.

One thing was abundantly clear: there was no expense spared toward the wellbeing of the birds. Stress, as it were, left a detrimental impact on the quality of the meat.

At that point, Fehlauer offered a gingerly nudge of the elbow, signaling it was time to head back out. But when I realized we were about to revisit the locker room, I was overcome with disappointment. Was this the end of the tour? I had just started to charge into a tirade of complaints—I did not fly all the way from Istanbul to be spending two minutes in a dark room with a gang of chicken catchers—when he laughed. As he did so, I began to appreciate that certain matters were getting lost in translation.

Fehlauer pointed toward a vacant cabin for what would be our second shower on site, before offering me a fresh set of attire. This second sterilization round was necessary to conform with the strict safety and quality controls that were in place and sought to avoid cross-contamination between different phases of the processing journey.

No sooner were we out of the lockers again than we found ourselves overlooking what appeared to be bath time for the birds themselves. Sliding down the rails, still upside down and hanging by the legs, the birds were momentarily submerged in water, then zapped with an electrical shock that—helped by the wet feathers—left them stunned. The shocks served not to kill the birds, but rather to render them unconscious—in line with industry, animal welfare, and other divinely mandated standards. I observed that this also served the practical purpose of aligning a chicken's jugular to an expectant blade further down the rail, making for a mercifully decisive slaughter.

From there, we followed the line toward the feather-picking area, where birds are dunked in scalding tanks to relax the follicles before the pluck. Fehlauer was now all but reciting the Portuguese tour guide booklet, as I struggled to discern his insights on how controlling the water temperature yielded the desired shade of yellow for the skin. *Does the color chart go from one to seven?* I thought to myself. It was a long shot at drawing parallels to the banana world.

Meanwhile, birds were rolling out of the scalding tanks at a rate of about one per second and continuing through defeathering machines that looked strikingly like the cylindrical rotating brushes inside a car wash tunnel. Watching feathered birds squeeze through the cylinders and come out stripped naked at the other end, so quickly and so efficiently, laid bare the state the carcasses were in. Whereas a second earlier, the chicken still looked like chicken—and, admittedly, evoked a sentiment bordering on *the poor little thing*—these naked *things* coming out the other end to be singed inspired feelings of a rather callous nature: a capitalistic feel-good factor. The birds had lost their identities. They were no longer chickens; they were now product. Barely a quarter of the way along the processing line, the metamorphosis from chicken to *cha-ching* was well on its way, and the corresponding emotional rollercoaster I had felt myself on, momentarily, came skidding to a halt.

Next up was the evisceration process, where another equally impressive choreography of mechanical maneuvers separated the offal from the carcass, starting with a quick swash to discard the preening gland that secretes feather-grooming oils. The cut is clean, inviting a penetrating bit that serves to widen the opening for a second ladle-shaped tool to scoop out the viscera. The hearts, gizzards, and livers are then split and go on their separate ways for further processing.

As we followed the line deeper and deeper into the plant, Fehlauer alternated gestures at the production schedule and the remainder of the line ahead of us. The product was now making its way through an increasingly complex labyrinth that catered to a diverse list of customer orders. It was these orders that essentially dictated what percentage of product would be packaged whole—as frozen broilers and grillers—and what part would be further carved, skinned, and deboned into boneless skinless half breasts, chicken wings 3-joint, and what have you. Here and there, byproduct would be collected to serve alternative industries. Leftover trimmings are minced, seasoned, and smoked to make frankfurters, while claws (or feet) are bulk-packed and shipped off to China. Bone and cartilage are labelled for pet food. Feathers head for the pillow manufacturer.

For Fehlauer and me, it was back to the lockers for the penultimate time. Stepping out of the shower, I was this time greeted with what could easily be mistaken for a space suit. A staff member was at the ready to help me slip into the outfit—circling me like a master tailor, putting and throwing and pulling at zips and flaps the length of me.

I looked across to Fehlauer, who was recognizable only by his voice when he spoke through a concealing layer of headwear, and learned we were about to enter the Further Processed Products (FPP) section of the plant. I stood opposite the closed doors overcome with anticipation, like Charlie at the great gates of Willy Wonka's chocolate factory. A buzzer sounded, and a pair of sliding doors brought into view a large, open area lined with all sorts of mixers and ovens and swarming with a crew of visibly sophisticated technicians in white robes. The scene resembled a clandestine lab more than it did anything else.

"*E é aqui que guardamos o molho secreto.*" I could sense Fehlauer grinning as he spoke from behind the face cover.

"Of course," I nodded. "The secret sauce."

This here was the place where novelties such as the *breaded chicken golden steak, cordon bleu,* and *chicken cutlets with spinach* are battered and breaded...concluding the production part of the supply journey from incubator to refrigerator.

CHAPTER TEN
ON CHINESE GOOSEBERRIES
AND OTHER CULINARY MISNOMERS

Bananas and poultry products made up the bulk of our sales, but they were far from being the only items we supplied. Chinese gooseberries, for one, were on display at many of our outlets.

But what are Chinese gooseberries, and why would anyone think to dig their teeth into a fruit carrying such an obscure name? It may come as a surprise to learn that we have all had them, and we all love them. We do not recognize the name only because marketeers want us to know them by a different, more appetizing, name: *kiwifruits*.

Culinary misnomers are a phenomenon in the food industry. Not unlike Jeep Wranglers, you start seeing them everywhere once they pique your interest. For instance, odd-shaped leftover chicken meat sells as *chicken nuggets*—with insinuations to a finer standard of dining. Add skin and you get *chicken tenders*. Chicken wings, as we saw earlier, were previously dumped because of the difficulty of mechanically extracting any meat out of them. Today, they are glorified as *Buffalo wings*—named after the city in New York state with historically the highest number of millionaires per capita.

Fish sperm and fish eggs are not items that one would naturally be swayed to pick from a menu, but *soft roe* and *imperial beluga caviar?* Double portion, please. European sea bass, once considered a holiday fish, has influenced fish nomenclature across Perciformes from as far west as Chile—where the Patagonian toothfish now goes by *Chilean sea bass*—to the Far East—where the old-fashioned-sounding barramundi is marketed as *Asian sea bass*. Most sophisticated diners would be hard-pressed to pick one up at the fish market if they saw them in a state of pre-fillet. Side by side, European sea bass, Chilean sea bass, and Asian sea bass look like they barely have anything in common beyond a pair of eyeballs and a dorsal fin.

Of course, the one that steals the show—the mother of all culinary names—is the coveted *Rocky Mountain oysters*, amounting to nothing more than a juicy pair of cattle testicles.

Back to our Chinese gooseberries.

Once demand for the lowly gooseberry exploded, helped by its new stage-name *kiwifruit*, securing a reliable supply source was no longer straightforward. Kiwifruits are farmed by different growers and in different countries, but none have managed to match the quality of the specimen supplied by Zespri International, the name carried by the kiwifruit producers' cooperative in New Zealand. Zespri's superior quality puts it in a league of its own, providing the organization with an advantage not unlike that wielded by monopolistic suppliers. And as is the case with any such scenario, the buyer's bargaining power—in this case, ours—becomes incredibly diminished.

Our unique value proposition toward our supplier partners—being reliable cold-chain operators with a presence stretching from Eastern Europe to Central Asia—was suddenly not good enough for Zespri, whose product we had been distributing in our markets. Where we insisted on sole distribution rights with such giants as Sadia, Dole, and Tyson Foods, that was simply not an option with Zespri, who were seeking to diversify their risks by having several distributors in every country. I met with Zespri's export director on a couple of occasions in a bid to secure exclusivity over their product, but there was simply no convincing him. While I do not recall the person's name, I do recall one fact about him that stood out. He was ranked first in the world on the amount of travel miles he racked up annually, owing to New Zealand's geographic isolation and Zespri's popularity with distributors around the globe.

CHAPTER ELEVEN
RED HERRING, RED APPLES, AND THE RED STAR

Jan-Peter Schøpp was a man of the world. A leading figure in the fisheries industry, he liked to plan his business trips from his basement man cave in Stavanger, Norway, where he displayed an eclectic collection of artifacts acquired from a life on the road. A visit to his bunker was as educational as a day at the museum. One came face-to-face with exotica ranging from the recovered keel of a Viking ship to a battle-hardened Papuan tribal axe—bloodstains and all.

But it seemed none of his adventures had quite prepared him for a business trip to Pyongyang. He was there to conclude the sale of Norwegian herring to the North Korean government. The price was right, as were the delivery conditions. The sticking point was an eleventh-hour amendment to the payment terms: "We will pay for every consignment two years after delivery."

"Two years?"

This was a far cry from the 30 days Schøpp typically extended to his customers, but the size of the contract was extraordinary as well: it gave him the exclusive right to supply pelagic fish to the socialist state's 25 million strong population. He was not prepared to let the largest sale of his career slip so easily. But no sooner had he objected to the term than he conceded the sucker punch.

"We'll be paying you in red apples." In the incredulous pause that followed, the North Koreans could sense the deal slipping away and threw in a sweetener to try and salvage it. "What say 80 percent red and 20 percent green. Does that sound about fair?"

In the business of supply, there is no obligation to be *fair*. If two competent parties willingly agree to a deal whose scope lies within the boundaries drawn out by the law, that was where the discussion on fairness ended. What is more important than fairness is the ability to give and receive consideration—be it product, service, or payment—in doses that serve the interests of both parties.

Schøpp left that deal on the table.

The first time I met Schøpp was in Stavanger in May of 2001. I had flown there seeking a supplier of frozen mackerel and herring (payment in dollars—100 percent green) to expand our own offering in the Caucasus. It emerged during one of our early conversations that he was as fascinated by the Silk Road as I was. It was a geography that had eluded him despite a lifetime of travel that took him to the furthest corners of the world. He shared the same yearning for the region that I did and was in the know on its economic upside. What he also knew—and I did not—was that a terminal medical condition made this opportunity his last chance to visit that part of the world. Perhaps he could even unearth a crowning relic to complete the collection adorning his man cave, where we were now sharing an ardent Nordic grog over conversation.

For Schøpp to complete his due diligence on our organization, I heeded his request to arrange for a tour of our distribution network across Turkey and the Caucasus later that month—after which we effectively sealed our partnership. I was looking for a regular supply of fish, and I found this most remarkable gentleman, whom I have idolized since, eager to supply us for the entirety of our geography on an exclusive basis. This came about despite him being under no obligation to offer such favorable terms, especially that his organization—Pelagic Partners—was in a comparably advantageous position to the jet-setting executive at Zespri.

The first shipment of Norwegian fish left Stavanger for Poti a few weeks later. Schøpp had come through for us. His willingness to supply us served to reaffirm the notion that in business, rapport and personal relationships are more powerful than the prevailing balance of power between supplier and buyer.

As with the sourcing of bananas and poultry products, securing a reliable and continuous source of fish comes with its own set of complex challenges. The underlying concerns are also very different for wild-caught fish than they are for farm-raised fish. For Schøpp's wild-caught mackerel and herring, the biggest challenge was in controlling the volume of fish taken out of the water each year so that the oceans remain healthily stocked. One intuitive response toward that end, drawn by governments in Europe and North America, was the introduction of fishing quotas. But as mackerel and herring are pelagic fish that crisscross oceans and seas, there was no mechanism to enforce any quota once a school of fish made its way into international waters or into the waters of a country lacking a quota system. Fish protected by Norwegian quotas in the autumn could well end up landed by a trawler boat along Spain's shores the following spring. For most of the rest of the year, the fish are in the high seas, where no government has jurisdiction over them. Treaties have since been put into place to regulate fishing along fish migratory lines in international waters, but they remain difficult to enforce.

Schøpp was an early proponent of sustainable fishing. Besides heading Pelagic Partners, he wore one hat as the head of the fish buyers' syndicate in Norway, and another as the honorary consul of Norway to Iceland—which provided him with a platform to influence fishery practices along fish migratory paths west of the Norwegian Sea. He explained to me that even within a country's own sovereign coastline, quotas—meant to limit the size of the catch a fishing crew could bring to shore—presented a problem: because one kilogram of large mackerel sold for more than one kilogram of small mackerel, smaller-sized fish (and any bycatch) were frequently released back into the water in the hope that a subsequent trawl yielded a larger specimen. Many of the smaller fish would not survive the catch-and-release; even worse, the larger mackerel that were targeted are of spawning age and taking them out of the equation so regularly was having a devastating impact on the wild stock's ability to reproduce. In effect, the quotas often did more harm than good, resulting in more dead fish and a lower reproduction rate with every new generation.

Another issue, which is closely related to (yet distinct from) the first, is that of defining a quantitative baseline for how a healthy wild stock is quantified. Marine biologist Daniel Pauly was one of the earliest to notice that every successive generation of fisherman would lament the good old days when the ocean's bounty was aplenty. This meant that the baseline for what represented a healthy stock was constantly changing with every generation of fishermen, leading Pauly to come up with the term *shifting baselines*. The volatility of this benchmark often yields a sticking point any time fishing quotas land on the negotiations table, with fishermen, governments, and environmentalists quarrelling over where to draw the line.

As with bananas and poultry, the future of the fish industry lies mainly in farming—specifically aquaculture. But where the banana and poultry industries have each narrowed down commercial-grade production to one or two hyper-efficient specimens (as Chiquita's Cavendish banana and Tyson Foods' Cobb500TM broiler), the productivity of fisheries is complicated by the wide variety of farmed species. The fish species that are traded commercially range from those that are aquacultured efficiently (to yield a favorable feed-to-edible-flesh conversion rate), such as Atlantic salmon and rainbow trout, to those produced so inefficiently that they really should not be on anybody's plate, such as bluefin tuna and giant tiger prawns.

In fact, some experts argue that some of the less efficiently farm-raised fish, also including the popular sea bass and cod, were initially farmed because they were in our faces as wild fish, and not for any methodically sought-out farming qualities. Despite advancements in science and farming techniques, the answer to questions like "How many kilograms of anchovies are needed to produce one kilogram of edible bluefin tuna meat" is still way above the 1 to 1 threshold needed to sustain the industry in the long run. In fact, for the aquacultured bluefin tuna commonly served at sushi restaurants, the conversion ratio stands substantially higher at around 20 to 1. In other words, for every 20 kg of anchovies fed to a bluefin over its lifetime, the yield is just one kilogram of edible tuna meat. By comparison, the feed to meat conversion ratios for Atlantic salmon and chicken stand at 1.8 to 1 and 2.6 to 1, respectively (when counting only the edible parts of the carcass).

Tuna bellies may hold some of the richest and best-eating meat the oceans have to offer, but their culturing is by no means sustainable with today's farming technologies and techniques.

To get confirmation on this, I visited a bluefin tuna farming operation in Turkey in 2004. I was permitted to dive inside one of the offshore pens housing these majestic beings—the largest reaching 800 kg, or the size of 10 fully grown men. Underwater, at a depth of 20 meters, I could see the tunas circling the inside parameters of the cage in uniflow, only adjusting their paths to avoid colliding with me. The fish swam at high speeds, but their confined manner emoted a wretched energy typical of a depressed, shackled beast.

At the farm, it was shared that a fish had to be groomed for up to 20 years before it reached a size that made removing it from the water any economic sense—a timespan that did not come without a heavy toll on both the environment and farming costs. I also learned that those were not the only challenges facing the industry.

Juvenile bluefin tunas are caught wild and transferred to closed pens built in the open sea. The practice diminishes wild stocks and disturbs the balance of the ecosystem as more and more of these predatory fish are taken out.

Additionally, large quantities of feed are artificially introduced into the sea where the pens are located, facilitating the spread of pathogens, and concentrating tuna waste in otherwise pristine ecosystems.

CHAPTER TWELVE
DROUGHT DISRUPTIONS

To complete our offering of fresh and frozen food commodities, we were still missing a critical product on our inventory list: butter.

Butter is a staple food item in considerable demand. It can be shipped and stored frozen and has a welcome shelf life of up to a year. I empirically gathered from the dozens of trips I made to the bazaars across Eastern Europe, the Caucasus, and Central Asia that there was a preference in our markets for the premium quality butter produced in Australia. I also knew that Australian butter was rarely offered across those markets, although I could not grasp why. In the end, I attributed the reason to the political and geographic divides separating Australia and the markets along the Silk Road.

In March of 2005, I decided to visit Australia—where I had spent the best years of my childhood—to explore butter sourcing options and study the logistical and financial viability of establishing supply routes to our region. As I made my way through the arrivals zone at Sydney Airport, a series of advertising boards were begging for my attention. "No Water, No Life," read one, the letters superimposed over an image of dramatic, arid wasteland littered with decayed cattle carcasses. "Every Drop Counts," another read. The messages brought back vivid memories from my childhood of a television spot that frequented Australia's television networks. It showed a rubber duck sitting in a bathtub, with the sound of water dripping as an echo formed around it. The message: save water.

My mood plummeted, and at long last, I realized why Australia was not exporting any of its butter: there was no butter. Not enough to go around, at least.

Fifteen years after I had watched those television ads, Australia was still fighting the same battle, and its adversary was only getting fiercer. The nation was now at the peak of what has come to be known as the Millennium Drought, the worst dry run to hit the continent on record. Low rainfall in consecutive years since 1996 was taking a massive toll on everything from urban households to agriculture.

One of Australia's largest and most reputable dairy producers was Dairy Farmers, a cooperative not unlike New Zealand's kiwifruit marketer Zespri, formed in 1900 when a group of 65 dairy producers merged to improve the marketability of their products. I met with Mark Felan, the cooperative's Commercial Director, at their new offices in Sydney Olympic Park.

Felan was a stubby man in his 60s who looked like he could have been a former Olympic shot-putter himself. He listened intently to my pitch and our journey along the Silk Road thus far, his body language showing equal parts excitement and restraint. When he finally spoke, he broke down for me the extent of the devastation brought about by the drought on Australia's dairy industry. Clearly, he was eager to get on board, but at the same time, his hands were tied because of curtailed supply.

Dairy production, and butter by extension, had been hit particularly hard by the drought. Farms were struggling to churn out enough stock feed, and there was simply not enough water to keep agricultural production running effectively; some crops, such as cotton, had completely collapsed. Still, we agreed to a pilot shipment, satisfied to establish proof of concept for the time being. If the shipment were profitable for both parties, we would use the experience as a steppingstone for a more sustainable form of cooperation once the drought let up.

Thus, despite the constraints, a first shipment of Australian *unsalted butter (82.5 percent fat content)* set sail to the port of Poti in Georgia two months later. The disruptions meant that the product could not be perfectly fulfilled to specification, but it still sold. A high potential venture now lay on the sideline—hampered not by demand, but rather by supply.

Interestingly, the root cause of the drought was the same El Niño phenomenon that threatened Ecuador's banana plantations at the other end of the Pacific Ocean. El Niño is a highly irregular system that lasts for years once it appears, and the ongoing cycle only let up in 2010 (by which time I had already exited the region). When the drought gave way, it brought not just rainfall, but a series of devastating floods that appeared almost overnight. The El Niño system had oscillated into La Niña—characterized by the cooling of surface seawater below normal levels. In effect, one was tempted to draw parallels between the impact of the El Niño and La Niña cycles on Australian produce and the prophesized seven years of famine that followed seven years of abundance in ancient Egypt.

My experience with Australian butter, though limited in scope, served to highlight another of the challenges that come with securing supply streams: nature. Whereby geopolitics and the power wielded by giant corporations could be negotiated, the environment is non-negotiable—an ever-present feature governing supply.

SECTION TWO
FROM GEOPOLITICS TO PETTY POLITICS

In the Bazaar of the Haberdashers, inside a raised stall, a group of backgammon players continued their dispute by the light of an oil lamp. Two dice went flying, followed by a curse and then a stifled laugh.

– Amin Maalouf, Samarkand, 1989

CHAPTER THIRTEEN
GEORGIA: CALLING POTI

The Republic of Georgia is strategically situated along the Black Sea, allowing it to act as a natural maritime gateway to the Caucasus and Central Asia. Bulky cargo transported by sea—including the fruits, meats, and other food products we supplied—arrives at Georgia's ports in Poti and Batumi before continuing its journey by road, rail, and often ferryboat to its destination.

Between 1999 and 2005, I came to know two versions of Georgia.

The first, that which preceded the Rose Revolution of November 2003, was a fantastically complicated and dangerous place. Despite the country's modest land mass, it was littered with breakaway regions and semi-autonomous zones. The most notable of these were Adjara, bordering Turkey (and hosting the port of Batumi), and Abkhazia and South Ossetia along the Russian border.

Georgia's security woes were not confined to its borders. A war raged in neighboring Chechnya, which abutted the country's Pankisi Gorge. Insurgents took advantage of the gorge's rugged terrain to stage cross-border attacks, exasperating matters. To the south, another territorial dispute between bordering nations Azerbaijan and Armenia had escalated into a full-out war. The guns were silent for now, but the continued absence of a permanent resolution made for a smoldering powder keg that threatened a testy ceasefire.

It was an unusually rough neighborhood, and it seemed fitting that The Mother of Georgia—a large aluminum statue standing high above the capital city of Tbilisi—carried a bowl of wine in one hand to greet friends, and a sword in the other to fend off foes.

The second version of Georgia I encountered—post-Rose Revolution—was a rapidly reforming nation that would soon find itself ahead of the curve on matters relating to security, governance, and ease of doing business. It was a rendition that did justice to the aspirations of the Georgian people, whom I personally found to be among the world's most cultured.

Our partner leading the operation in Georgia was Fady Asly, a larger-than-life character whose gigantic stature was amplified by a baritone voice and a forthright personality. I got my first introduction to Asly from reading an interview-based article where he compared himself to Asterix, the eponymous comic-book hero who leads a small band of Gauls against the invading army of the Roman Empire. Asly presses his case to the interviewer by revealing he had suffered multiple bullet wounds while running a citrus distribution business during the Lebanese Civil War. But where Asterix succeeded in staving off the Romans by means of a magic potion, Asly counted on sheer courage and hard-headedness to survive Georgia's perilous security situation. In addition to being our partner in Georgia, Asly provided oversight for our operations in Azerbaijan and Armenia. He also served multiple terms as the president of the American Chamber of Commerce in Georgia (AmCham Georgia), which provided him a platform to drive market reforms and speak out against corruption.

Georgia held significant importance to our organization as both a distribution center and a transit hub. I therefore saw it fit to visit the capital Tbilisi and the port at Poti at the earliest opportunity, which came in December of 1999.

When I first landed at Tbilisi's Novo Alexeyevka International Airport, as it was known at the time, it was just after midnight. My trip was planned on extremely short notice, and I had not taken the time to arrange for advanced airport pickup and hotel booking. This was in line with the modus operandi I adopted at the time to optimize travel flexibility. The plan was to arrive at the airport, grab a hotel flier or two for lodging ideas, and make my way to a hotel by airport taxi.

Fig. 3 Map of major seaports along the Mediterranean Sea and the Black Sea.

Before long, though, I would learn that proceeding as such in Georgia made for a very uninformed—even foolish—decision. To make things worse, I was sporting a look that, in retrospect, made me appear both outmoded (even by '90s standards) and suspicious: a pair of ragged corduroy pants, a black leather jacket, and a woolen hat that looked like a repurposed balaclava. My attire, my profile as a young man of Middle Eastern origin, and the fact that I had no airport pickup or hotel reservation combined to raise the eyebrows of airport immigration officers—already on high alert to filter out militants on their way to the Pankisi Gorge, and hence to the front lines in Chechnya.

At passport control, a sullen immigration officer examined me from head to toe before proceeding to question me.

"Why are you here?"

"I'm visiting on business," I responded.

"And what is your business?"

"I supply bananas," I said, deliberately saying as little as was necessary to avoid any misinterpretations.

"Bananas? Don't think you are smart, and I am not." He countered. "Who is waiting for you at the airport?"

"No one."

"Where are you staying?"

"I don't know yet. Where do you keep the fliers?"

It was more than he wanted to hear; at that point, I could tell it was going to be a long night. An interrogator whisked me away to a detention room, barely wide enough for a single wooden stool. I was now seriously intimidated and worried about the growing prospect that my profile as a supply professional would be misconstrued for a Pankisi-bound militant.

The questioning went on all night, with two security agents—playing good cop, bad cop—going down every conceivable interrogation line. Almost 12 hours into the ordeal, they finally let up. My passport was stamped, and I could enter the country. I landed on a flier and made my way to the Victoria Guesthouse, where I slept through the rest of the day and into the next morning.

The following day, fresh and recovered, I was picked up from the guesthouse by Imad Bekai, the head of our sales team in Tbilisi. He arranged to take me on a tour of the market, which was built around the central Dezerter Bazaar and a dozen smaller neighborhood markets. The concept of the supermarket was barely making its way into Georgia, and the few outlets that operated under the modern format reserved a symbolically small space for groceries; most consumers were accustomed to bargaining and distrusted the fixed prices mandated by supermarkets.

This archaic market structure had an obvious implication on how we approached distribution. Rather than a complex network of routes and sales points scattered across the country, our logistical effort was predominantly focused on deliveries from our main warehouse to the central bazaar. On the periphery, we operated several outlets through agreements where we provided store-operators with product handling training and covered their store rental fees in return for the exclusive representation of our products. Finally, larger sales to wholesalers were conducted through our warehouses at the outskirts of Tbilisi. The system not only worked, but it also made us leaders in the banana and poultry meat markets. It was a model we replicated across different parts of Georgia, as well as in Azerbaijan, Armenia, Kyrgyzstan, and Kazakhstan.

My first stop with Bekai was naturally the Dezerter Bazaar— Tbilisi's largest outlet. Legend has it that the bazaar, a legacy agrarian market that caters directly to individuals and small-scale traders, takes its name from a band of deserting soldiers who arrived at the spot to sell their arms in the 1920s. Nowadays, of course, one was more likely to encounter legs than arms, with our Tyson leg-quarters (that sold in 15 kg cases) among the prime attractions. One also saw many of our Dole banana cases—many of which were reused by vendors for storing locally-grown produce. The large indoor section of the bazaar was lined with open table displays of chicken, fish, pork, fruits, vegetables, and other local produce. An outdoor section exhibited mostly non-food items that could better endure the elements. Though happening, the scene was much smaller in scale to that at Istanbul's Bayrampaşa Hali, where wholesalers arrived with trucks and trailers to procure several tons of product at a time.

At first glance, Bekai did not strike me as someone who would stand out in a crowd. But arriving at the bazaar, I quickly saw that first impressions can be misleading. Feisty and street-smart, he was like nothing more nor less than the motor driving Dezerter Bazaar—screaming orders at staff and customers alike in a rudimentary mix of Georgian and Russian, assigning quantities and prices. Once we finally made it to our outlet inside the bazaar, a stream of people suddenly appeared—right on queue—to cart away case after case of Tyson leg-quarters, Sadia broilers, and Dole bananas. It was too good to be true, as I soon realized: the scene was set up by Bekai, playing the puppet master, to impress me with his sales prowess. That is not to discredit Bekai; it was nevertheless remarkable that he could orchestrate such a procession. Equally impressive were the intelligence briefings he received through the grapevine on the state of the market.

Bekai's act was one I would see play out time and time again when I returned to Dezerter Bazaar, accompanying suppliers and prospective partners in the coming years. Another familiar face that often accompanied us on those tours was that of Gela Mtskhvetadze, a young policeman who was hired to escort Bekai and the daily sales proceeds to the banks. A striking feature of our revenues was the means in which payment was collected: it was all cash. Because the nature of commodity trading put a heavy reliance on volume, a substantial number of Georgian lari banknotes made their way from the bazaars and our warehouse to the banks daily.

As the port of Poti played such a crucial link to our supply flow, I braved the 350 km drive from Tbilisi to observe our logistical infrastructure there on the third day of my trip. It was the first of many visits I would make to the port city, my itinerary often including stops at the port, our offices and the two large warehouses we operated there.

The scope of our logistics in Poti was extensive and broad. In addition to receiving, storing, handling, and distributing product, it entailed arranging for transit shipments to our other markets in the Caucasus and Central Asia. The person overseeing that effort was Sharbel Aoun, with whom I liaised daily. Despite the pressures of the operation, Aoun carried himself with an imperturbable sense of positivity and wore a congenial smile that radiated reassurance. On several occasions, I would hitch a ride with him to Poti, riding in his Lada Niva—the Russian Jeep—while a cassette tape of Nirvana's *Unplugged in New York* alternated from side A to side B for the entirety of the six-hour journey. The Nirvana in the Niva not only made the drive tolerable; it was a statement on how far we had come from the days of the Cold War.

All in all, the going was rough, but it was good. Until it was not.

CHAPTER FOURTEEN
A MURDER

Being on the road in Georgia was not without its risks.

During one of my visits to Tbilisi in the summer of 2000, I was invited to take part in a football game that was organized for company staff. The game ended well into the night, and Bekai, accompanied by security escort Mtskhvetadze, offered to drive me back to my lodging at the Sheraton Metechi Hotel—the only hotel with an internationally recognizable name in the country at the time.

We were approaching our exit along the main boulevard running parallel to the Mtkvari River when a black Volga vehicle sped by us, then cut us off. A tinted window came down, revealing a man waving us down with a gun and gesturing toward the shoulder of the road.

We cooperated and stopped the car.

No sooner had we done so than four men, all dressed in black and waving guns, approached us. Mtskhvetadze, who held a police badge, stepped out of the car to negotiate while Bekai and I remained in our seats.

I was not sure what to make of the situation. Was this expected in Tbilisi? Were these gangsters or undercover cops? Could Mtskhvetadze's police badge or Bekai's street smarts get us out of this?

For answers, I fixed my gaze at Bekai—who had gone mute—and tried to analyze his body language for any sort of hint. Ominously, the only reading I could decipher was telling me he was as terrified as I was. Things were not looking good. Clearly, we were in a situation that even Bekai saw as random, unpredictable, and dangerous.

A few moments later, I made out Mtskhvetadze handing over some cash to one of the gunmen. He was then free to step back into the car. As we resumed our drive to the hotel, not another word was spoken. Mtskhvetadze too looked shaken, which got me thinking we were lucky to have escaped unharmed.

In the larger scheme of things, we did get away unscathed, yet the incident could easily have escalated into a violent climax. The significance of the event for me was that it foreshadowed a treacherous path as we pushed our allegorical trade caravan deeper down the Silk Road. In Georgia especially, our journey would be plagued with petty gangsters and organized criminals who sought to extort our gains. We—along with other businesses in Georgia—would endure hardships and relentless racketeering up until one November day in 2003, when the Georgian people rose to scream "enough"—a spontaneous movement that culminated in the Rose Revolution and the tearing down of a corrupt legacy system practically overnight.

But for one person, the revolution came too little too late. It was only a few short months after our road misadventure that we suffered our first serious security incident in Tbilisi. In October of 2000, Bekai, Mtskhvetadze, and a driver were making their way from the Dezerter Bazaar, hauling away the cash proceeds from the day's sales. As was his habit, Bekai stuffed stacks of cash inside several of his pockets to mitigate the risk of pickpocketing, and he scribbled the amount that was on him on the palm of his hand with an ink pen. As they drove through a deserted street, their car was stopped by an armed gang.

They were ordered out of the vehicle. Mtskhvetadze was instantly and summarily executed on the side of the road.

The bandits then turned to Bekai, demanding the money. Bekai, impulsive and hardheaded, at first refused to acknowledge there was anything on him. He took a beating for it, and it was only then that he proceeded to hand over portions of the cash. It was a risky game he was playing—not unlike Russian roulette—as Mtskhvetadze's corpse lay next to him on the ground.

The amount Bekai gave up did not match the figure he had earlier scribbled on his hand, but in the heat of the moment, the bandits failed to make that link. It was a lucky escape. The fact that Mtskhvetadze—the only person carrying a weapon—was murdered, coupled with how the bandits knew to specifically extort the money of Bekai, indicated that the crime was not a random one, but one planned and executed on specific surveillance and intelligence.

Mtskhvetadze's premeditated murder came as a shocking development to everyone who knew him. It provided a sobering reality check on the gravity of the dangers we faced in the field, and a true test of our commitment to the journey. If there was ever any doubt, the incident only strengthened our resolve to persevere. For abandoning our path now would have seemed a great betrayal of our colleague, whose life would not be lost in vain.

CHAPTER FIFTEEN
A KIDNAPPING

On the morning of June 7, 2001, I was on a routine call with Aoun trying to work out the feasibility of distributing Turkish lemons in Georgia. On the other line, I had Marino Trastullo, an agricultural engineer on our team, from whom I was trying to extract the cost of goods.

"It comes to about $12 a crate." Trastullo was speaking with a heavy Italian accent.

"Does that include loading the container and export formalities?"

"No, no, no. That's $12 sitting at the storage cavern here in Anamur."

"Are you saying that's the cost prior to even packing?" I asked. "We can't really work with that. Do you think you can work out the total up to the point of loading?"

"I can have it by early this afternoon. Let me call you back then."

A few months earlier, we had decided to venture into local produce. The idea was to source and package locally grown fruit—primarily bananas and citruses from Anamur and other towns in Mersin Province—for sale in Turkey and abroad. Trastullo was recruited to lead that effort. He had spent the past decade or so working the banana plantations across the Dominican Republic for one of the large corporations, making him an ideal candidate for the role. Trastullo was a *bananero* at heart and had met his Dominican *bananera* wife at the plantations outside Santo Domingo—where they likely exchanged vows underneath a banana tree. But despite his technical expertise, I could see that he had little patience for the business end of things.

Upon hearing back from Trastullo, I tried making another call to Aoun to conclude the exercise we had started that morning, only to discover that his phone was switched off. It was uncharacteristic of Aoun, or anyone else in fruit operations for that matter, to turn off their phone—especially during office hours. I kept trying him, but two hours later, Aoun remained inaccessible. I tried reaching Asly, the head of our organization in Georgia, but he was not taking any calls.

I could sense at this point that something was not right. Raw thoughts of Mtskhvetadze's murder came rushing to my head. Just then, I received a frantic call from Nahas, confirming Aoun had gone missing.

Over the next few hours, the news started trickling in. Aoun's Lada Niva was found, deserted along the same road where Mtskhvetadze had been killed. The window closest to the driver's seat was smashed in from the outside and the Nirvana cassette tape was rolling with nobody in the vehicle. There was no trace of blood or empty bullet cartridges at the scene, which was welcome news. But there was no sign of Aoun either. From that moment on, the incident would be treated as a kidnapping.

There were suddenly a thousand questions begging to be answered. Was Aoun really kidnapped? If so, who did it and what was their motive? And of course, there remained the most important question of all—the one nobody dared to ask: was he still alive?

Aoun's kidnapping hit us like a bolt from the blue. It was a development that none of us were prepared for, least of all his wife and two little girls. The incident shook everyone who knew him to the core, and we were left to puzzle over if and how we could seek his release.

At the time, we represented food giants Dole Fruits and AJC Food, and had maintained, to a certain degree, our relationship with Tyson Foods. This meant that except for Sadia, our largest supply partners were all American-owned organizations. In that way, our business represented American interests by extension, and Aoun's kidnapping was a direct attack on those interests.

Our first reflex was to therefore try and leverage America's political weight in the country to secure Aoun's release. While the volume of American product we moved fell significantly short of that generated by larger industries as defense and oil and gas, it was still enough to get the members of the US Embassy in Tbilisi actively involved in the case.

It was easy to establish contact with the embassy for a couple of reasons. First, Asly was the president of the AmCham Georgia. Second, as a rule of thumb, we made it a point to hire the same law firms used by the US Embassy in each of the countries where we operated. This yielded a credible liaison for the establishment of communication channels if needed.

We also consulted with Frank Sánchez, the advisor who had earlier moderated our strategic retreat at the Çırağan before delivering his sapient keynote aboard the *Hiawatha*. Sánchez was closely associated with Dr. Roger Fischer—founder of the Negotiation School at Harvard and author of several bestsellers on the topic of negotiations—and had a stellar track record as a negotiation expert himself, including having played a key role in concluding the Brasilia Peace Agreement that ended a centuries old dispute between Peru and Ecuador.

But it would ultimately fall to Asly to call the shots on any play made toward executing the negotiation—if there was to be one.

The strategy devised for a prospective negotiation to secure Aoun's release was built on three pillars that had to be executed flawlessly: relationships, communications, and concessions.

The first of these, relationships, entailed acquiring a deep understanding of who the kidnappers were, how they were organized, and what motivated them. While the gamut of potential kidnappers was broad, perpetrators ultimately fell under either of two groups: amateurs, such as street thugs and petty gangsters, or professionals, such as organized crime syndicates. The two groups behaved in markedly different ways.

Amateurs, being inexperienced, posed a significant mortal risk on the abductee's life. This risk only increased with time, as the kidnappers became increasingly restless to end the ordeal. Panic brought on by nervousness or paranoia could quickly escalate with potentially adverse implications for the victim's safety. Those same pressures, however, made amateurs prone to reducing their demands as the ordeal protracted, with the ransom dropping by the hour or—at the most—by the day. This would come about because amateurs lacked the financial and infrastructural means to hold on to a victim for extended periods of time. If Aoun had indeed been kidnapped by such a group, the culprit could really be anyone, and we could expect to hear the demands almost immediately.

Professionals, on the other hand, displayed an entirely different set of behaviors. The kidnappee is in safer hands (albeit relatively) owing to a paramilitary-grade organization with centralized command and the discipline to sustain the ordeal endlessly. Because professionals were under no rush to start—let alone conclude—a negotiation, their demands could grow over time. If Aoun was taken by an organized crime syndicate, then it was very likely that that group was one of only a handful operating in Georgia or in one of the country's semi-autonomous enclaves. It also meant that it was very unlikely we would hear from the kidnappers within the first 48 hours after the abduction.

Our first task was figuring out which of the two groups Aoun's kidnappers represented. We got our first clue when several days went by with no contact from the kidnappers—indicating that they may be in complete control of the situation.

Another line in our investigation had us searching for precedents in Georgia. And there was one: the case of two Spanish businessmen who were kidnapped 8 months earlier. In fact, the pair had still not been released, despite the establishment of communication lines between their families and the kidnappers.

We now had two indications to go by that we were indeed to be dealing with professionals.

As far as communications (the second pillar of our strategy) went, there was one important guideline. There was to be no uncoordinated interaction between the abductee's family or company staff and the press. Any show of emotion—inevitable by a close relation—would be interpreted as a sign of weakness, something that could reinvigorate the kidnappers' resolve during the negotiations. This was a massive ask especially of Aoun's family, and something that would become increasingly difficult to hold up as the ordeal stretched on.

Furthermore, we expected Bekai to be the person the kidnappers reached out to first, owing to his visibility as our head of sales in Georgia. He was provided a detailed brief of what he could and could not say should the kidnappers contact him. The most important directive was that we would not be negotiating before we could establish proof-of-life—evidence that Aoun was alive and well. Proof-of-life also proved beyond any reasonable doubt that the person placing the call was indeed connected with the kidnappers.

It must be said, however, that the real communications masterclass was the one delivered by the kidnappers. One full week after Aoun's disappearance, there was still no word from anyone. The silence was numbing, and we were left to analyze, reanalyze, and then overanalyze what that implied. If amateurs had been behind the kidnapping, it was surely bad news. We were now pinning our hopes on it being the pros behind the act. Proof-of-life would have to be established before we could make sure of that.

The script provided for Bekai to follow was very specific in terms of what constituted proof-of-life. We wanted the kidnappers to provide an answer to a secret question, one only Aoun could supply. This was designed to avoid a scenario in which we would receive a finger, or perhaps an earlobe, in the mail—a practice that was not alien in the abduction space. The secret question was left for Aoun's wife to ponder over. She came back with, "What was the name given to the dog Sharbel owned back in Beirut?" If the kidnappers respond in time with Dusty, then we were in business.

The third element of our strategy was related to concessions, specifically the conditions under which any would be made. This included guidelines that ensured every concession was reciprocated adequately, and that every compromise was smaller than the one preceding it. These rules were designed to ensure that the conditions for any agreement remained reasonable.

Twenty-nine days had passed since the kidnapping with still no word. Our hopes of ever seeing Aoun alive were getting dimmer by the day. Then, on day 30, our desperation was eased. Bekai received an anonymous call from a person claiming to represent the kidnappers.

"We have Sharbel. If you want to see him again, prepare one million laris in cash and await further instructions." This amounted to just under $500,000 at the day's exchange rate.

"Don't waste my time and yours." Bekai was in his usual combative mood. "If you really expect me to take you seriously, let me hear his voice."

"I can't do that."

"Fine then, provide me with his dog's name and we'll take it from there."

"Dog's name? What dog's name?"

"I said it once, and I'll say it again," Bekai retorted. "You're wasting my time. And yours. Buzz me once you have the dog's name."

"Sure. I'll get you a dog's name, but that's going to cost you 50,000 laris." Despite his best efforts, Bekai could tell he was out of his league. Before he could respond, the caller delivered the drop-off instructions and abruptly hung up.

The effort we put into planning our concessions was designed to give us an edge over the kidnappers over the course of the negotiations. Now, we realized that our adversary was at least as prepared to engage as we were. The anonymous caller had either anticipated our proof-of-life request or had devised the reciprocal request for the 50,000 laris on the fly. Either way, it showed expertise. Delivering proof-of-life was a valuable concession—and there were to be no free meals on the table.

The money drop was made in broad daylight. Bekai himself

placed a briefcase next to a public bench and watched as a man picked it up and walked away. It was adjudged that interfering in any way would have put Aoun at risk. The contents of the briefcase, however, were not the requested 50,000 laris, but rather a smaller amount that should have been sufficient to keep Aoun nourished during the ordeal. It was playing hardball.

Incredibly, another 29 days passed with no further word from the kidnappers—let alone the dog's name. This period would prove harder than the original 30 days, as doubt crept in whether the caller truly represented the kidnappers. Perhaps it was an opportunist, seeking to fool us out of the ransom money. Perhaps the kidnappers were no professionals, but amateurs all along—a case of a robbery gone bad, a shooting, and a discarded body.

The wait time taught us that for the victim's family and friends, a kidnapping is in many ways harder to endure than death itself. Death offers closure. People mourn and learn to live with their loss. Dealing with a kidnapping, on the other hand, is like fighting a cancer with a 50 percent survival rate. It could drag on for months or years, throwing the lives of the victim and their kin in limbo as they are left to suffer and guess at the ordeal's outcome.

At this point, 59 days into the kidnapping, Aoun's parents, wife, and daughters were temporarily resided at the Ortaköy Princess Hotel near our offices in Istanbul. With nothing more than a phone call to show for the last two months, they were emotionally on edge and understandably volatile; at one point, they flew to Georgia unannounced and reached out to the kidnappers through statements to the press, complicating our unified communications drive.

At our offices, the mood was sour and disheartening—the kidnapping dominated every facet of our daily lives. It appeared as if everyone were suddenly an expert at kidnap negotiations, and many fantasized about how they would have reacted if it had been them, and not Aoun, at the scene.

On day 60, Bekai's mobile rang for the second time. He immediately recognized that it was the same voice as 30 days earlier.

"You'd better have that dog's name."

"It's Nestor. Now let's get serious."

There was a long pause, before Bekai asked the voice to repeat the name.

"Nestor, NESTOR! Nestor like Nescafe—"

To Bekai's disbelief, the caller was unable to deliver Dusty's name. There was no point dragging on the conversation. Bekai hung up, and it looked like we were back at square one.

When the news reached our Istanbul office, Nahas and I immediately made our way to Aoun's family at the hotel to deliver the updates in person. We braced ourselves to receive the wrath of a family that we tried to sideline in the quest for their son's release; we were now preparing to tell them that we did not even know who held him, let alone if he was still alive.

We gathered at a corner in the lobby. Not wanting to mince words, Nahas laid down the news.

"Look. I'm not going to lie," he said. "Whoever was on the phone was a hoax. He came back with Nestor. Now, I know—"

But before he could finish his sentence, the family erupted with euphoria. "He's alive, he's alive! Sharbel's alive!"

Nahas and I looked at each other—speechless, confused, and delighted.

"Wait. What happened to Dusty?" I asked Aoun's wife.

"Sharbel had another dog that he called Nestor; you didn't know that?" She reached to hug her daughters, tears of relief pouring out of her eyes.

It was just the type of communication mishap we had so meticulously planned to avoid, and it threatened to complicate the resumption of negotiations with Bekai hanging up on the caller earlier.

"We need to get the kidnappers back on the phone!" I scrambled to call Bekai on my mobile.

On August 24—78 days from the kidnapping and 17 days since contact was last made with the kidnappers—a raid was conducted by a special law-enforcement unit on an abandoned compound in the Pankisi Gorge. It was an intervention captured by camera crews in a sensationalized clip broadcast to the nation. Toward the end of the act, a camera follows a General as he approaches a ragged, bearded figure. He removes a blindfold, revealing a barely recognizable Aoun. The beaming General then proceeds to throw his arms around Aoun, who was once again a free man.

No ransom was paid.

A week into the kidnapping, the absence of a call from the kidnappers had compelled us to work on the assumption that the perpetrators would be known to the authorities. Accordingly, we opened a second front by launching a media campaign advertising Aoun's face and the word "Kidnapped" on billboards across Tbilisi. Along with carefully worded press releases, this succeeded in pressuring the government to act against the kidnappers and to make Aoun's release a priority for law enforcement agencies.

In the end, a strategy built on relationship management, communications, and concessions had worked, though not without several close calls and not without frustration. The important thing was that it had worked, and Aoun was released, alive and well.

CHAPTER SIXTEEN
MIKE'S AZERI GAMBIT

In parallel to the events unfolding in Georgia, a different saga was playing out further east, in Azerbaijan—the largest of our markets in the Caucasus. While the capital Baku served as the main theater for the drama, the curtains for the opening scene were being raised 5,000 km away, in Paris, France. With the dear reader's permission, I will turn the clock back to October of 2000.

Dr. Motta, Nahas, and I were gathered at the world famous SIAL Paris Food Fair when the glass door to our booth suddenly swung open. A middle-aged man from the Caucasus barged in, uninvited. He was modest in stature and carried himself with an air of arrogance and entitlement. The intruder, who appeared to know exactly who each of us was, fixed his gaze on Dr. Motta.

"I'm here to tell you that Sadia can only continue operating in Azerbaijan if you drop these guys," he declared, gesturing at Nahas and me. "Let me take care of your distribution, and I'll hand you the *monopole* on a silver platter." It was thus far making for a highly amusing scene, an almost welcome distraction from the tedious pace of affairs at the fair. But before any of us had time to react, the man served up a second, more personal, and more brazen threat.

"Chalabi's life is in your hands. He needs to pack up and leave Azerbaijan immediately."

Mike Chalabi, the subject of this Paris threat, was our partner heading the distribution of frozen meats and fresh fruits in Azerbaijan. I had first made his acquaintance the previous year. He had planned our rendezvous over an authentic Azeri lunch at a historic restaurant nestled within Baku's old city fortress walls. In his fifties, Chalabi was tall and tidy. When he spoke in English, a posh British accent cast above an immaculate three-piece dress ensemble—a volatile marriage of contrasting patterns, held together by virtue of their grading increments. When he conversed in Arabic or Turkish, he did so with an eloquence he owed to his grandmothers, whose bloodlines traced back to Iraqi and Turkish royalty. Still, he had a propensity for shyness which turned his face flush-pink at the faintest of provocations.

Despite a 30-year age gap, I would easily establish rapport with Chalabi, who had spent part of his youth in my hometown of Beirut and was a fellow alumnus of the American University there. He was a man who had experienced several ups and downs in his career. Nahas once confided to me that he had a poker tell on his financial situation. "When photos of his wife appear regularly in *Hello!* magazine, that's an indication that his chips are up. If she's absent over several issues, it's likely that he's in financial trouble. That's the litmus test."

I was meeting with Chalabi that day to discuss our growth strategy for Azerbaijan and to get an update on the situation in Turkmenistan and Uzbekistan—two potentially lucrative markets east of the Caspian Sea that had remained out of our reach.

"Our friends over there are ready to receive our chicken, but we still have to figure out a way to get paid in the absence of a foreign exchange market," he said, as a waiter placed two cold ones on our table. Pale lager was Chalabi's beverage of choice. "Cheers, old chap." He raised a pint in my direction, maintaining eye contact as he gulped down half of his drink in the inaugural sip. He rationed the other half, savoring it over the entirety of his meal.

Business in Azerbaijan was good. Despite the evolving standard of living and a legacy Communist vibe, the country had many riches to offer the hapless romantic, not the least of which was cultural. Among the land's hidden gems, tribal Caucasian rugs stood out, splendid in their natural dye colors and geometrical designs, as did the Beluga Caviar, freshly harvested from the Caspian Sea, and considered by many a connoisseur to be of the highest grade anywhere. The economy was only expected to expand once the oil— which could be seen seeping out onto the ground in some areas, as if calling to be extracted—started flowing to the world's markets upon the completion of the Baku-Tbilisi-Ceyhan pipeline.

As with the other markets in which we operated, our group pioneered the supply of bananas and, later, frozen chicken leg-quarters to Azerbaijan. Our warehouses and distribution lines covered the whole geography, including the enclave of Nakhichevan, a noncontiguous region separated from the mainland by arch-enemy Armenia. But the prevailing mentality in Azerbaijan around the turn of the millennium was largely Cold Warish. Beyond the oil and gas sector, very few foreign companies were there on business. Our presence as foreign distributors operating locally was therefore not overly welcomed by our competition. In true Communist fashion, they were hellbent on monopolizing the banana market and later the frozen poultry market.

Hence the threat against Chalabi delivered to us at the SIAL Paris food fair. Even before then, Chalabi had complained of an increasingly systematic campaign of harassment targeting our local operation. Additionally, our competition was alleged to be dodging customs duty, making it ever harder for us to compete. Our customs duty formalities were also taking longer than usual, with a detrimental effect on our supply streams and on the quality of our perishable products. This suggested that the party behind the racketeering campaign held a degree of political influence. The only thing keeping them from expelling us out of the country outright was, again, our positioning as representatives of American interests. The whole Caucasus region was fast gaining strategic prominence as far as the US was concerned, largely owing to the oil and gas reserves in the Caspian Sea. Even though bananas and chicken could not hold a candle to oil and gas, the general premise held that if anyone were permitted to tamper with US agribusiness without consequence today, then they would surely be emboldened to mess with oil and gas interests tomorrow.

Despite the pressures we faced in Azerbaijan, there had been nothing to date to suggest a risk to the safety and security of our team on the ground. Things changed after the Paris incident as a series of threats followed in quick succession. The escalation compelled Chalabi and his trusted accountant to make for London, England, for a month-long break just before Christmas. As this was our busiest period of the year, I decided to fly out to Baku to cover for Chalabi. What followed was 30 climactic days of untold provocation.

The temperature was close to freezing when I landed in Baku that December. The city's only international hotels at the time, the Hyatt Regency Baku and the Park Hyatt Baku (housed in the same complex), mainly catered to businesspeople and were eerily quiet because of the holiday season. Accordingly, Chalabi recommended I avoid those hotels and opt for a short lease on an apartment along the Torgovaya, a relatively happening strip along Nizami Street in the city center, which I did. The apartment was sufficiently prepped for the winter months despite its worn-out rugs and a gas combustion heater that evoked a fear of a house fire more than it did a longing for snug chimney-side soirees. I stretched my back on a large worn sofa, staring straight up at the ceiling to discover cracks that were wide enough to spy on my upstairs neighbors. Before I could process the sight fully, and barely three minutes into my rental agreement, the door buzzer rang.

Great, I thought, *must be a welcome-to-the-community cake from the neighbors.*

I opened the front door and there stood a man, dressed in an intimidating black leather jacket and a fur ushanka ear-flap hat, presenting me with a $1,000 electricity bill.

"Abi, ben şimdi taşındım..." I protested, explaining that I was just starting my tenancy and that he should take the matter up with the landlord. I proceeded to hand him a note with the owner's number and forced the door shut.

But the man was not satisfied. He placed his finger on the buzzer and kept it there as I hesitated to reopen the door. Five or ten minutes later, the buzzer still going, I relented. This time, I used the door chain to secure the door ajar and fired an angry tirade that convinced him to finally walk away. As I headed back to reclaim my place on the couch, the buzzer went off again.

My adrenaline level shot up as I turned around, swung the door open, and prepared to let out another salvo of insults. But to my surprise, the man in the ushanka was not there. In his place stood a woman, perhaps in her sixties, waving a similar piece of paper.

"Evet?" I asked, straining to make sense of this twist in the tale.

She handed me the bill, pointing to a figure of $800—this time in water utility charges.

I was flabbergasted by this surreal development. *"Bir saniye lütfen, parayı alacağım,"* I said, slanting the syllables to lend my pidgin Turkish an Azeri accent. I asked her to wait, pretending I would dutifully fetch the cash.

"Yahse," came the affirmation, as I shut the door gently, with the lady fully expecting me to withdraw 8 crisp greenbacks from the safety of my bosom. Instead, I headed straight for my suitcase, which was still packed. Grabbing it, I walked back past the expectant woman and headed for the exit—sacrificing the month's rent. I proceeded to hail a taxi and headed to the Crescent Beach Hotel—a local accommodation along the coast of the Caspian Sea.

Staying at that apartment was clearly not going to end well. While it cannot be established with complete certainty, I had a hunch that the harassment served by my two early visitors was indeed related to the broader racketeering campaign against our organization. The party behind it wanted me to know that they had eyes on me.

On the business front, the security threats were paralleled with a damaging banana price war with the competition. Because of the perishable nature of bananas, we could not afford to hold back our sales until market prices shot up again—the alternative to selling fresh bananas today was, figuratively speaking, to sell banana soup tomorrow. Our partner Dole, who had been supplying us with large quantities of bananas to support its own Banana Wars, was now concerned at how low our sales prices were dropping in Azerbaijan. And, while no one stood to benefit from the rapidly falling sales prices, it was looking like our competition had the stamina to see this fight through until they secured their *monopole*, aided by what we suspected were favorable import-duty levies. That disparity in levies meant that our competition would still be breaking even, while our finances sunk deep into the red.

About a week into my stay in Baku, banana prices continued to drop daily. We were now losing upward of 30 percent on every trade, and a line had to be drawn somewhere. In banana distribution, the market leader has the most influence over setting market prices, meaning a position of leadership comes with the added perk of a higher profit margin on every sale relative to the competition. This, of course, is contingent on the age and condition of the stocks held. In a sense, every other player was at the mercy of the market leader when it came to pricing and profitability. It was therefore crucial for us to maintain the highest share of the market in Azerbaijan— but the losses we were incurring were providing a threat to that status quo.

I put in a three-way call with Nahas in Istanbul and Chalabi in London, and we agreed on a play. I would visit the competition at their headquarters and tell them in no uncertain terms that we were never quitting Azerbaijan, even if we never profited an Azerbaijani manat. The visit would be a show of defiance and perseverance. It was a long shot at ending the price war, but the reality was that we had nothing to lose.

The next morning, I asked Saeed Yasser to set up a meeting with the competition. Yasser, a medical doctor by trade, oversaw our sales effort in Azerbaijan and knew his way around town. He was astounded by my request. "That's suicidal!" he protested. "These guys are dangerous." But his protests fell on deaf ears.

As we drove through the gates into our competition's premises, I was bewildered by the size of their storage and handling facilities. Lining the yard were at least six dozen container trucks loading and unloading cargo. The warehousing area went on for hundreds and hundreds of meters. The operation was huge—for the first time, I wondered if perhaps we were not out of our league. Besides their fruit and poultry distribution business, our competition was said to operate several other food commodity *monopoles*.

Nevertheless, the course was set, and I would see it through as best I could.

We reached the office area; I stepped out of the car, and a short, stout man approached me. As we shook hands, it quickly dawned on both of us that this was not our first encounter. I had seen his face before, and he had seen mine. It was the same person who had served us the threat to Chalabi in Paris.

He introduced himself as Serdar. I made him out from his accent to be Turkish, and not Azeri. Turkey was now my home, which provided a good talking point for building rapport to dispel the overriding tension. We spoke about the charm of Istanbul, life in Baku, the food fair in Paris, and the nightlife in Beirut. It was an odd meeting, in sub-zero-degree Celsius weather, standing in a cargo yard amidst the beeping sounds of reversing container trucks and the smell of gasoline-powered Soviet-era forklifts.

Small talk over at last, he asked why I was there.

I reached into my jacket for two Villiger cigars, and we each lit one up. "Listen, Serdar. I grew up in Beirut, in a conflict zone," I started.

"Yes?"

I was keen on making a statement. I wanted a line that expressed truth, but also one that spoke of guts, vigor, and business acumen—all the while resonating a measure of *esprit de corps* with this formidable adversary. But most of all, it had to mask the bluff. Critically, anything I said could not be open to interpretation as an attempt at price-fixing—an illegal practice with even bigger implications on our reputation that was to be avoided at all costs. I had prepared my statement as I lay in bed the night before and rehearsed all morning at the Crescent Beach Hotel and in the car. That day, our price war had sunk our selling price of bananas to $13 a case, while our costs were at least 150 percent that.

"Serdar," I went on, "you and me, we understand each other. Tomorrow, it's a new and beautiful day."

With that, I walked back to the parked Volga, where Yasser was waiting. As we drove away, I set my mind to assessing my performance of that morning and came away trusting that standing up to Serdar's bullying in that way would have sufficed to convey to him that we were indeed prepared to go the distance in this fight. At the very least, he must now be second-guessing himself on his decision to persevere with the price war.

The next morning, I asked Yasser to hike up our selling price from $13 to $22 a case—a fair price that put us just above our break-even point at the current cost structure. Word was passed to our main cold stores in the city of Sumqayit (35 km outside Baku), from which the bulk of our wholesale transactions were executed.

A few hours into the trading day, Yasser rushed into my office.

"Serdar is still at $13," he lamented. "How am I supposed to sell now?" He was overcome with panic, with good reason. "Let's drop our prices, these guys are not responding."

I shook my head. "Let's follow through and hold at $22. Perhaps they have ripe stocks that they need to clear out before raising their prices on the fresh arrivals."

Later that afternoon, when sales would have slowed down almost to a halt, we got word from the market that Serdar was trickling his prices up to $15. By the next morning, he was at $18, which was still not high enough for us to conclude any noteworthy sales at $22. Our stocks continued to age meanwhile—the banana soup cauldron brimming over at Sumqayit.

It took another couple of days before Serdar finally pushed his prices up to $21 a case. Our customers could now afford to buy our product at $22, paying a small premium for the Dole label. Things appeared to be getting back on track, in time for the fresh arrival of cargo aboard the *M/V Crown Ruby*. The consignment was now on its last leg, a railway journey from Poti to our cold stores in Sumqayit.

The following day, Yasser was jubilant.

"Serdar is at $24!"

"That's fantastic," I said. "Let's get the goods from the *M/V Crown Ruby* customs cleared ASAP. We're in for a killing."

But of course, there was a hold-up.

Someone at customs was delaying our transaction—48 hours passed, and our goods were still not cleared for release. As a result, our warehouses became depleted of any notable stocks. In the meantime, Serdar was enjoying a temporary *monopole* and his sales price was still increasing—now at $30 a case. I could feel my guts wrenching as I connected the dots. I decided to pay the customs house a visit myself to sort out the delay.

Customs worked out of a typical Soviet-era building. Joined by Yasser, I took a couple of stair flights up to the department of the officer in charge of our file. It goes without saying, we were asked to wait. About thirty minutes later, the officer finally showed up, flanked by three junior staff. He wore an effervescent smile and a uniform with gleaming shoulder insignia. A thick grey moustache served the dual purpose of overstating his authority and downplaying his big, arched nose.

We got straight to business: he did his best to poke holes at our import documentation, and I did my best to prove him wrong. I was mindful of the need to reconciliate my arguments with face giving measures that ensured his prestige remained intact—not least in the view of his spectating subordinates. In the end, I was made a promise that our product would be released without any further delay, respecting all protocol.

As we prepared to part, I reached out my hand to the officer. Our palms connected in a firm and resolute handshake as our eyes got caught in a staring contest. At that moment, the officer blindsided me with a most unexpected parting gesture. With our hands still locked, he pierced his middle finger into my palm, compromising my manhood in the process. It was a subtle maneuver that nobody else in the room could see or sense, but it spoke loudly about his intention toward releasing our shipment.

In that instance, everyone in the room assumed our bananas would be released that day, except for two men, who knew that we were—in fact—going to hell. One other person, sitting a good distance from the scene, must have foreseen this conclusion. The price of his bananas was shooting up to $33 a case—in time for the New Year's Eve buying spree.

The day following my encounter with the customs was New Year's Eve. To mark the occasion, The Crescent Beach Hotel was advertising a seated dinner party, to be held at the main restaurant area. I called reception and booked the last available spot. When I arrived at the venue later that night, I found that I had been allocated a place at a table that seated ten people. There was a small problem; the remainder of the seats were occupied by the same party of nine Azeri friends. They had planned to party together, and there I was forced to share their round table, sticking out like a sore thumb. After an awkward attempt at exchanging smiles and niceties, everyone on the table went mute and I accepted that this marriage was not for the best.

I walked out of the restaurant and made my way to the hotel's deserted beach area, from which I could make out several floating oil rigs under the glare of the moon. I lit up the last of the cheap Villiger stogies from my impulse buy at airport duty-free—which I was saving for New Year's Eve—and lay on the sand to reflect on the week's events. Van Morrison's *Moondance* was playing through my Sony Discman, which I collected on my way to the crescent shaped shoreline.

I was in this curiously wonderful land, on the Silk Road proper. But the mysticism of the place appeared perverted by corruption and extortion, and there was no guarantee for our continued presence here.

My mind drifted back to the incident where I had the palm of my hand tickled by the officer. *It's not all bad*, I found myself thinking. *Surely, this depraved act was driven by a sense of frustration. An admittance of defeat.* At that, I suddenly realized that we still stood every chance of securing our banana shipment from customs. Just then, my newfound cheer was disrupted when my mobile rang. It was Yasser.

How nice...

"Yasser, Happy New Year, my friend!" I said enthusiastically.

But his response was faint beneath the crackling of the strained cellular network, and he was spacing out his words. "I'm dying," he said. "I'm calling to say goodbye."

"What?" I gasped. "Where are you? What happened? Are you OK?"

"I'm dying, that's it, you can't save me."

"What's wrong with you? Are you having a heart attack? Wait, was it Serdar's men? Did you call the emergency response services? Do you want me to call them?"

I was bombarding him with questions. But he was offering no answers, only repeating, "No one can save me now, I'm dying." He hung up.

I suddenly realized that Yasser was the only person in Baku whose number I had, so I proceeded to call Chalabi in London. The mobile networks were heavily overloaded by a spike in usage I attributed to New Year's Eve celebrants, but I still managed to get through after several attempts.

"Mike, I'm cutting to the chase. Yasser says he's dying, I'm not sure what happened to him."

Chalabi was chuckling at my perceived panic. "He'll be all right in the morning. Don't you worry about him, he's always like that."

"Always like what? He sounds like he is fighting for every breath. The guy is dying. This is serious!"

"I have known Yasser for years. Trust me, he will be all right. You have yourself a great New Year's Eve celebration."

It was one final loop along the emotional rollercoaster to sign off on the year.

Crestfallen, I pinched at my cigar and flicked it into the Caspian Sea. It barely breached the surface before reappearing, its foot still smoldering. As another wave hit, I dared not look to see if its flare would not be extinguished—as it lay afloat above 50 billion barrels of flammable oil.

The next morning, Yasser showed up at my hotel for breakfast looking completely rejuvenated. *What a difference a day makes,* I thought. Yet another day passed, and our bananas were released by customs.

A couple of weeks later, Chalabi returned to Baku and I made my way back to Istanbul. In the aftermath of the Paris threat, we had used our influence with the embassies in Ankara, Tbilisi, and Baku to stymie any attempt at carrying out a physical threat against Chalabi or any of our other team members. The message was received loud and clear: we would not be muscled out of Azerbaijan. This prompted Serdar's group, who were also hurting from the price wars, to approach us with a proposal. For a fixed monthly payment, we would be assured a 50 percent share of the banana market. For another larger payment, we would get 30 percent of the frozen chicken market. All customs duty taxes would be deductible from those payments. Furthermore, we would collaborate on distribution to optimize operational costs and selling prices. Serdar and his backers would also ensure that we were no longer harassed.

Chalabi and Asly took charge of responding to the proposal. They analyzed the strategic, practical, and legal aspects of such a deal. Chalabi appeared hesitant to enter such an arrangement. He was pushing for a different approach for conducting our business in Azerbaijan, by way of redirecting our sales into the country through wholesale middlemen from the port of Poti. Asly appeared more bullish about the deal, even as he compared it to "selling our soul to the devil." He argued that the proposal, in addition to being commercially lucrative, provided a security cover for Chalabi and the rest of our team.

After several weeks of legal consultations and negotiations, an agreement was reached in February. The security threat on Chalabi, however, continued to escalate. A few months later, the racketeering peaked when his Jeep Cherokee disappeared, only to reappear a couple of days later compressed into a cube of steel. By August, American political advisors signaled that they were downgrading their outlook for the entire Caucasus region, expecting the business environment to worsen once the oil started flowing. In Azerbaijan, specifically, most foreign enterprises were being pressured to leave, the only exception being the large oil and gas corporations and their respective contractors.

Thus, by August, our deal with the devil collapsed.

Immediately afterward, Chalabi wanted out—blaming the sustained harassment maelstrom. The timing of his exit, right after the agreement collapsed, was met with varying reactions from within our team. There were those who believed that he had been too close to the fire for too long, that he understood the potency of the threat wielded by our competition best. But there were also those who speculated that he was offered a stake in a business interest in London, where he would be reunited with his family.

A few days later, Nahas and I were rushing to board a flight at Istanbul Atatürk Airport when he suddenly stopped at a kiosk and reached for a *Hello!* issue on display.

"Is this really the best time?" I asked, as he began to claw at the magazine's transparent polybag.

"You want to know if Chalabi got his own sweetheart deal? Look no further," he said, proceeding to flip through the tabloid's pages for a photograph of Chalabi's wife. Of course, she was nowhere to be found.

CHAPTER SEVENTEEN
ORGANIZATIONAL BICEPHALY
IN ARMENIA

The last of the countries in which we operated in the Caucasus was Armenia—an isolated nation in the true sense of the word. Geographically, Armenia was completely landlocked, with no direct access to a seaport. Politically, it was mostly cut off from bordering Turkey and Azerbaijan because of longstanding feuds. As a result, the reigning sentiment among Armenians, once their nation was left to stand on its own two feet following the collapse of the Soviet Union, was one of vulnerability. The lay of the land inherently stunted any prospects for meaningful economic growth, making Armenia the smallest of our markets in the region.

Most things Armenians cared for appeared to be teasingly out of reach. For one, Mount Ararat—a sacred national symbol said to be the landing site of Noah's Ark—lay just beyond the border with Turkey. Yet, the mountain remained ubiquitous in Armenian everyday life. Also, claims of a 1915 genocide suffered at the hands of the Ottomans remained short of global recognition, despite acceptance as fact by political heavyweights the United States and Russia. Even the oil riches of the Caspian Sea appeared to forsake

Armenia as they flowed through three bordering countries at a tantalizingly close distance. These letdowns, captured in song, poem, and folklore, were woven into the fabric of a society that had become hauntingly dependent on nostalgia for morale. The nation sought to heal itself by turning to culture and intellectualism, reinforcing a legacy of Soviet heritage. Every office and home in which I would set foot in during my travels there provided supporting testimony by way of a piano, a private library, or both.

My first trip to Armenia was in December of 1999. Travel restrictions at the time meant that to get from Istanbul to the capital Yerevan, I had to fly to Georgia and continue my journey southward by car. The first half of the road trip—the three-hour stretch from Tbilisi to the Armenian border—made for a bumpy affair. The road, technically an international highway, was nothing more than a dirt trail. One got the impression that the Georgian government left it in that condition to appease Azerbaijan and Turkey, with whom they shared interests in the Baku-Tbilisi-Ceyhan pipeline. In contrast, the second half of the journey, that which covered the segment of road from the border checkpoint to Yerevan, was truly world-class and served up a statement of stubborn defiance.

Our distribution network in Armenia did not escape the country's lethargic pulse, either. It was a sleepy operation, configured around 450 tons of rented reefer storage space and 11 containers that we used to store and ripen bananas. We operated wholesale and retail space at the main bazaars and used our vans to cover the 20 or so small minimarkets dotting the capital. Our presence in Armenia was, for all intents and purposes, cosmetic. If we had ever isolated our Armenia operation from the rest of the region, the returns would not have justified the effort and the associated risks. By planting our flag there, however, our profile as a regional player grew in clout. This in turn dealt us a stronger hand in supply-side negotiations.

As with our other markets in the neighborhood, we had to overcome endemic challenges here related to customs formalities and *contrabanda*, product theft, and volatile exchange rates. We also struggled to compete with a powerful oligarch who was seeking to dominate the market with imported poultry to add to his growing list of *monopoles*, including those in agricultural commodities. But unlike anywhere else, I discovered on my first day in Yerevan that our operation suffered an additional self-inflicted burden of an existential nature: a poor leadership structure. Ironically, the issue was not a lack of leadership but, rather, too much of it.

At the helm of the organization, we had two feuding country managers who made no secret of their animosity toward each other. It was a freakish chain of events that led to this situation: one country manager had been hired to replace another, but a legal loophole complicated the firing of the first. The resultant state destabilized every facet of the operation, from company culture to distribution. But because our venture in Armenia represented a small fraction of our business, the issue was never deemed a priority at the group level, and the status quo was left lingering. The outcome was an enterprise comparable to a bicephalic sloth in a state of embryonic diapause; effective decision-making was prohibited, and growth was stunted.

The warring heads of our Armenia operation could not have been any more different in character. In the red corner was Khachig Bakalian, a stalwart ideologist upholding austere principles. Baron Khachig, as most people knew him, carried himself with a flair of old-school pragmatism. His calm and collected nature lent him the aura of a wartime General. Those who worked under him spoke of a man's man.

In the blue corner was Jean-Michel Wehbe, a playful, nonchalant empiricist whose main concerns hovered around muscling Baron Khachig out of the company and winging the rest of his tenure with as little effort as was necessary. In fact, both Baron Khachig and Wehbe were on their final stint before retirement and were fighting tooth and nail for the right to see out their mandate.

When I first stepped into our Yerevan offices, centrally located in Yerevan's Nor Nork district, my presence was interpreted as a rare visit from headquarters upon which rested the future of our leadership structure in the country. Neither Baron Khachig nor Wehbe could shake off an overriding paranoia as they went beyond the call of duty to press their respective cases for the top job. No sooner had I pulled out a duet bench by the piano near Baron Khachig's desk than he initiated the proceedings against Wehbe, who had just happened to make his way to the office brandishing a sharpened lead pencil and notebook.

"Jean is a real parasite," Baron Khachig began. "He's added no real value since his arrival and our overheads have only doubled since. He barely understands the market and only shows up at the office for a couple of hours every day!"

I was taken aback by the brazen claims, which Baron Khachig had made no attempt at keeping from Wehbe—seated opposite me. For his part, Wehbe remained ice-cold and began to scribble Baron Khachig's every word in his notebook, only pausing intermittently to look up at his adversary. It was his way at hitting back.

When Baron Khachig was done talking, he turned to Wehbe, finally acknowledging his presence.

"Jean, why aren't you shaved today?" he shot.

At that, Wehbe put down his notebook and turned his attention to me.

"See that?" he said, gesturing to a table flag on Baron Khachig's desk. "That is a political flag. His partisanship is the reason business is suffering. We're alienating customers who are opposed to his political views." Wehbe paused for effect. "Also, why don't you ask him what he's got behind those folders?" He was now pointing his pencil toward a dram of whiskey that Baron Khachig was nursing discreetly.

I was in Armenia to assess our supply and distribution operations—seeking to identify performance gaps that we could improve on. Instead, I was getting dragged into office politics and personal feuds. Rather than let myself get drawn too far in, I cut the gathering short and asked Baron Khachig and Wehbe to join me for dinner that evening. I hoped that might defuse the day's tension and allow us to talk business in a more relaxed setting.

At dinner, it was confirmed that Baron Khachig's beverage of choice was whiskey. I broke the ice by asking if he had a favorite.

"It's all whiskey," came the response, in—it must be said—a whiskey voice.

"But you must have a favorite."

"Let me put it this way. I don't have a favorite, but I do have a strategy."

That piqued my interest as I attempted to hide a curious smirk. I had always maintained that a person's beverage of choice spoke volumes about their personality. To be presented with a strategy took it to a whole different level.

"The first pony is always a Johnny Walker Black Label," he explained, with growing pot-valor. "I savor the taste and appreciate the aromas. When I'm done with that, my taste buds are too numb to make out any more notes, it would be foolish to carry on wasting Black. So, I switch to the cheaper Red."

Truth be told, it was a pragmatic answer.

But to my dismay, where Wehbe was concerned, I discovered that—despite a plethora of vices—he was, in fact, a teetotaler. That realization threw me off the rails. Any attempt at an assessment of his character would certainly lack a measure of credibility or depth on my behalf. It is not that I do not trust an abstainer, but rather that I could not fully trust my own judgement of one, robbed of my quirky means for assigning a character to this personality bucket or that.

As the evening evolved, I understood how Baron Khachig and Wehbe worked "together": the two had learned to symbiose. While not explicitly acknowledged, they had synchronized their circadian rhythms so that they would completely avoid each other at work. Baron Khachig played the early bird, showing up at the office as early as 6 AM. Wehbe, on the other hand, played the night owl, ending his days at the warehouse and our bazaar outlets at 4 AM. He would then head to bed, before waking up late in the day—long after Baron Khachig had made his way back home.

Despite all the noise, I was able to get down to the specifics of our operation over the next couple of days. The three of us identified several areas for improvement, mostly related to our marketing efforts, logistics, and sales nodes at the bazaars.

One of the flagged issues concerned the inflated rents we were paying for our main warehouse. A meeting was set up with Bedo Badalian, the proprietor of the facility, in the hope of renegotiating our rental fees. Cold storage space was difficult to come by in Yerevan, which gave proprietors an edge in negotiations. To his credit, Badalian had shown loyalty over the years and resisted advances by our competitors to upend us.

The Badalian meeting was set for 5:30 AM at the warehouse premises. In preparation, we had readied a presentation outlining our vision for the future of our relationship. I was dressed in a suit and tie, hoping to project a favorable image.

Badalian, in a show of respect, had asked his team of five or six staffers to be present at the meeting, which would also be attended by Wehbe. He only made his entrance after everyone had found their seats around the large table dominating an old, poorly lit meeting room. Badalian was a big, stout man, his shirt untucked and his hair unkempt—the very personification of a Eurasian Brown Bear. He was loud and cheerful, and carried a large bottle of vodka in each hand as he walked into the room. In close pursuit were two more men carrying a heavy cauldron of *khash*—a local hangover cure, concocted of bovine hooves left to simmer overnight—in preparation for our cockcrow conclave. I had never heard of *khash* before, and it only took a quick look at the delicacy to confirm that it would be of the acquired taste variety. Protocol necessitated I roll with the ravenous appetites in the room, so I made no objection as Badalian raised his glass to make a toast, setting off a chain reaction of *Nasdrovia* salutes running clockwise around the table.

It must have been close to 9 AM, over three hours into our meeting, when I finally suggested to Badalian that we get to the business end of things. The cheer was instantly sucked out of him. I had all but insulted him, I realized, and hastily acted to salvage the situation by raising my glass to make another toast. The mood pendulum swung again, and the entire room erupted into a fit of laughter, then another round of toasts. At that point, one thing was abundantly clear; business would be left for another day. Or perhaps, this was business, Yerevan style—where personal relations trumped all else, not least the presentation on my laptop and the tie now safely tucked away inside my pocket.

Granted, our sales turnover in Armenia was modest, with profitability hovering around the break-even point for much of the time. But, all things considered, our presence served its intended strategic purpose: it solidified our proposition as the only truly regional distributors in the Caucasus. Baron Khachig and Wehbe both remained in place for a while; they were tried-and-true individuals, which was an especially sought-after trait in a cash-intensive business as ours. Matters only escalated when Baron Khachig and Wehbe's squabbling would begin to reflect on our relationships with international suppliers, whom I occasionally accompanied on routine market visits there.

In May of 2001, Nahas and I decided to visit Armenia together. It would be the only journey he ever made to the country. One of the objectives we set ourselves for the trip was to assess whether the hierarchical status quo was sustainable in the long run. If we adjudged it to be otherwise, we would then have to agree on who was best suited to lead the operation forward.

By then, the Armenian national carrier, Armavia, had secured the rights to fly a direct route to and from Istanbul. We purchased our tickets, which committed us to a seven day stay—there was only one scheduled trip per week—and prepped ourselves for the short, overnight flight.

When we landed at Zvartnots International Airport, we were pleasantly surprised by the facility. It was considerably larger and better conceived than any other airport I had visited in the Caucasus or Central Asia. And yet, there were barely any airplanes on the tarmac. There was no doubt that such a grand terminal, in the absence of a booming economy, would have been a remnant of Armenia's legacy as a member of the Soviet Union.

As we made our way to passport control, we were directed to fill out our customs declaration forms. Because we were flying in from a hostile nation—everything Turkic was generally anathema to Armenians—it was essential that we were made to suffer the full wrath of immigration's bureaucracy. Thus, it would be a full hour before a single passport control officer finally showed up—decorated in Soviet-era fatigues, a long coat, and an impeccably groomed grey moustache. The officer looked like he was singlehandedly keeping alive the spirit of the Cold War. I signaled for an American passenger I was chatting with to pass ahead of me, a gesture rooted equally in courtesy and lab-rat experimentation.

The General, laying his eyes on the American passport, was now doubly irritated. In his mind, this American *pendos* was flying in from Turkey to ransack what was left of Armenia's economy. Some tense eye contact followed, after which the American was finally asked to make his way back to the end of the queue.

"What's happening?" I asked, as he passed me.

"He says he doesn't like my handwriting," came the amused response. It was a classic East-meets-West encounter.

Nahas was to become the second passenger struggling to make it past passport control, but for a whole different reason. We had come here to decide on the future of our Armenia operation—to take a good look at our leadership team, the distribution infrastructure, and the market—and he had already come to a verdict.

"I've seen what I need to see," he said. "If we don't fly back to Istanbul on the same flight, we're going to be stuck here all week."

"You've seen what you need to see?" I laughed. "We're not even past passport control!"

"Listen," he said. "The airport gives this place a great façade, but everything else probably needs to be built from the ground up. This market reeks of opportunity. You could sense that looking through the airplane window from ten thousand feet up. I say we hold our position here for good."

"We know it reeks of opportunity," I contended. "That's why we came here in the first place. To be pioneers, to revive the ancient Silk Road." I smiled, deliberately adding, "The Golden Road to Samarkand! But let's do this the right way. Let's look at the data afresh, revise our strategy and straighten out our leadership team. Any decision we take needs to be sound and calculated, derived from a carefully prepared feasibility study."

Nahas, now showing his trademark restlessness, shot back with a one-liner that I have long considered his magnum opus: "I don't believe in having a feasibility study; I'd much rather a *visibility* study." He proceeded to point in the direction of a vending machine standing against a wall. "You see that bottle of Coca-Cola in there? That is all the confirmation we need that this market is ripe for the picking." Nahas' thinking was along the lines that a Coca-Cola presence in Armenia demonstrated a strong American commitment to Armenia's economic development from the highest echelons in Washington, D.C.

"And if we do maintain our operation here, who do you suggest head it?" I asked.

"New blood," he said. And that was that. Nahas left and I stayed behind to execute.

CHAPTER EIGHTEEN
BISHKEK BARTER: SWISS TRUFFLES FOR YOUR TIN CAN HERBS

In early 2000, we were at another crossroads. The time had come to decide on the future of our distribution operation in Kyrgyzstan, a country situated deep in the heart of Central Asia. Kyrgyzstan was one of only two Central Asian republics with a foreign currency exchange market at the time—the other being Kazakhstan. Revenues collected from the sale of American chicken leg-quarters and Brazilian frankfurters in Kyrgyzstani soms could be traded for American dollars, which could in turn be used to pay our suppliers and complete the cycle of trade. In the absence of a currency market, the alternative would have been to barter for other fungible commodities—an obviously impractical dynamic on which to build a modern-day organization.

Kyrgyzstan was our smallest market in terms of revenues generated. A multitude of reasons made it so, but three stood out.

The first was a modest economy, curtailed by limited government spending and the absence of substantial foreign direct investments. This in turn constrained purchasing power across Kyrgyzstan's ethnically diverse consumers, who were also struggling to adopt an enterprising mindset following separation from the USSR in 1991.

The second reason was shipping constraints. Because the country is landlocked—situated a thousand kilometers from the nearest seaport—it was impossible for our high-grossing bananas to survive the prohibitively long transit times. A banana leaving the port of Guayaquil, Ecuador, turned into soup long before it reached our facilities in Bishkek. Our sales in the country were therefore limited to frozen meat products.

Finally, Kyrgyzstan presented a cashflow problem that constrained the volumes we could commit to the market. A typical leg-quarter sailing from New Orleans, LA required at least 75 days to reach Bishkek. This held true whether the product transited through a port along the Black Sea, the Mediterranean Sea, or even the Baltic Sea further north. It typically took another 90 days to flip the product and receive payment from the moment it arrived at our distribution facilities. The capital put up for procuring product could hardly be recovered before a cash-to-cash cycle time of six months had elapsed—a terrible deal by any standard.

Still, Kyrgyzstan represented our last bastion in Central Asia. We had earlier exited the more lucrative market in Kazakhstan because of a dispute with a partner. While it was true that our sales in Kyrgyzstan were low—with very little growth potential—we held on to the prospect of leveraging our infrastructure there as a platform for transit sales to markets in neighboring Kazakhstan, Uzbekistan, Tajikistan, and Mongolia. As time passed and those prospects failed to materialize, however, we needed to give serious thought to whether it made sense to continue our operation.

Oversight for our Central Asia operations in Istanbul fell to Laura Meade, a seasoned market veteran with an entrepreneurial flair and a mastery of workplace politics. Having experienced the faltering of our thriving venture in Kazakhstan firsthand, Meade had become disillusioned with the entire region nestled between the Caspian Sea and China. Moreover, she was not a proponent of Raymond Smayra, who was entrusted with heading our operation in Kyrgyzstan. As the debate over our continued presence in that market became more polarized, it was she who spearheaded the *leave* campaign.

There remained a gaping hole in the credibility of Meade's argument—and everyone else's, for that matter—for exiting Kyrgyzstan: besides Smayra, no one involved in our frozen poultry trade, Meade included, had ever set foot in the country. Until someone's boots were on the ground, any decision we would take remained largely unsubstantiated. To remedy this, I saw it fit to fly to Bishkek myself.

I made the first of two trips to Bishkek in May of 2000. As I disembarked from my Turkish Airlines flight at Manas International Airport, making my way down a set of mobile access stairs, I was overcome with a feeling of having stepped through a time warp into an abandoned era. This was vintage Silk Road. Besides a boneyard of abandoned Soviet aircrafts—foretelling of a forgotten city—there appeared to be no other commercial jets on the airport apron. Indeed, there was no terminal building in sight. Several dozen people were congregating at the base of the aircraft, amongst a marching band. They were there to welcome the person debarking ahead of me, who appeared to be a local tribal chieftain. Once he was on the ground, the procession started to move, and in the ensuing chaos, I followed closely behind for a couple of kilometers on foot—assuming it was heading for the terminal building. But rather, I found myself arriving at a parking lot instead, where the tribal leader and his devotees hopped in their cars and drove away. I was already outside the airport premises, passport unstamped, luggage unclaimed. It was now beginning to sink in that Bishkek was truly like no other city I had visited. I made my way back to the tarmac and managed to locate a tiny room designated for arrivals, where I was greeted by our Smayra.

"I thought you missed your flight!" he said.

"What is this place?" I asked, looking around at the empty room. "Where's passport control? Where is everyone?"

"Everybody's left already," he replied. "We're going to have to get your passport stamped at the ministry."

Smayra was in his late fifties when he joined our organization. He brought with him a wealth of experience acquired distributing products as varied as tobacco and pharmaceuticals, and he had operated in places as far and wide as Cyprus, Ukraine, and Mongolia. He was a humanist who never lost the common touch; his silver curls, long sideburns, and puffy eyes earned him the moniker *Tom Jones*. But a year into his tenure at our organization, Smayra had still not registered any meaningful wins on the ground. On most days, sales failed to exceed a few hundred dollars. This prompted Meade to procrastinate on supply deliveries—further choking Smayra's ability to cater to demand in what was now a perfectly vicious cycle.

My immediate goal in Bishkek was to gain a full understanding of the market's dynamics. There was very little data to go by, which meant that I would have to gather and rely on my own empirical findings. I enlisted Vladimir Petukhov, who was our lead salesman and Smayra's right-hand man, to plan a comprehensive tour of the market. I requested that the itinerary cover all the city's hotels, restaurants, and major supermarket chains, which typically represent a significant portion of our client base.

But when Petukhov returned with a schedule, there was only one hotel on the list: the Hyatt Regency Bishkek—where a Swiss sous-chef bartered homemade chocolate truffles for rare herbs and spices grown on Smayra's terrace in old tin cans. There were also just two restaurants that fit the modern sense of the word—Navigator and American Pub. The country had no supermarkets, let alone supermarket chains. Most retail transactions occurred via a network of bazaars and shops. Osh Bazaar was the largest of the capital's markets, where a large indoor compound housed food commodity retailers and an open area was lined with stalls for abacus-wielding vendors pushing livestock and other consumables. There was also an entertainment section: a trailer the size of a 20-foot shipping container housing a single-screen cinema. Inside, Bruce Lee's *Enter the Dragon* looped throughout the day.

The business landscape in Bishkek was at once promising and disheartening. Its raw, virgin economy suggested opportunity—a pioneer's wonderland. Yet, the ravaged state of the economy curtailed any prospects for growth. As with the other former Soviet Union economies, the fall of communism—a system that theoretically barred private commerce—and the ensuing metamorphosis toward a capitalistic blueprint endowed Kyrgyzstan with the promise of an economic boom. But where most of those states could build on the oil and gas of the Caspian Sea to usher in a socioeconomic renaissance, Kyrgyzstan remained rudderless in its search for a catalyst to jumpstart its economy.

This reality was stumping our growth and, in turn, reflecting badly on Smayra. In addition to his Tom Jones handle, he was now affectionately dubbed the Van Cleef of Central Asia—an allusion to the famous jeweler—because his sales volumes were closer to ounces and carats than they were to the containerloads and metric tons to which our industry was accustomed.

On my penultimate night in Bishkek, Smayra and I met up for dinner at Navigator. Smayra was enjoying a White Russian cocktail, for which the joint was famous. I peered down at his drink.

"Would you say that your glass is half-full or half-empty?" I asked, with a pondering gaze.

"That's exactly it," came the reply. "When you come to do business in a place like this, you park your pessimism at the door." He smiled faintly, before adding "We simply can't run on the fundamentals; we have to look to future potential. The numbers mean nothing."

By then, I had acquired a sufficient understanding of the market, and the subtle slam on Meade's attitude told me that Smayra and I were on the same page. We could pull off Kyrgyzstan if we saw the glass as half-full.

The next morning, we gathered to sketch out the beginnings of a business plan to boost growth and profitability. We broke the problem down into two parts, covering the demand and supply sides of the equation. Each part was then assigned sufficient resources for due diligence.

On the demand side, we were concerned with finding ways to increase our wholesale figures in Kyrgyzstan and establishing cross-border sales avenues to neighboring countries. Logistically, this scoped the movement of product from our central warehouse to our clients across the region. To achieve this, there were several levers at our disposal: we would set up points of sale at Orto Sai Bazaar and Alamedin Bazaar, which, combined with Osh Bazaar, formed the city's three largest markets. We would also expand our distribution network to cover the country's second largest city, Osh, as well as

Lake Issyk-Kul—a popular tourist destination that hosted several resorts and spas. Finally, we would grow our fleet of distribution vans to extend the reach of our product to retailers scattered across the main cities.

To support this expansion drive, I put forward a recommendation to transfer Walid Sakalaki, a rising star on our team, from Antalya, Turkey, to Osh. Osh was strategically important, as it acted as the main sales transit point to neighboring Uzbekistan and Tajikistan owing to its proximity to those countries. Sakalaki had previously completed a stint in Poti. That experience made him technically competent for the job. Also, he spoke both Russian and Turkish, the two languages essential for doing business in the region.

On the supply side, the challenge was to redraw our supply routes to enable faster, cheaper, and more regular product deliveries from our suppliers to our central warehouses in Bishkek. This was a complex undertaking, because any route would eventually have to combine road, sea, and rail modules. It necessitated a highly collaborative effort with our supply and logistics partners, which would have to wait until I was back at our Istanbul headquarters.

To date, we had been using the port of Poti for deliveries to Kyrgyzstan. The issue with that route was that product had to transit via Georgia and Azerbaijan, before traversing the Caspian Sea by ferry to Turkmenistan. It then continued its journey through Uzbekistan and Kazakhstan, before finally reaching Kyrgyzstan. With each border crossing, we lost precious time. Furthermore, we had no way to track a shipment in transit beyond making phone calls to border stations in the hope of receiving any sort of update.

Once back in Istanbul, I rolled out a map of the shipping world and proceeded to examine the potential routes at our disposal. The most critical part of any route would be the port of arrival once product left the Americas—at which point cargo would be consolidated and readied for transit to Bishkek by rail. The rail segment of the journey, from the port of arrival to Bishkek, provided a particular constraint: quantities would have to be shipped in multiples of 160 tons, which was the capacity afforded by a single train segment consisting of four adjoining cars. Even this minimum quantity was significant for a market the size of that in Kyrgyzstan, requiring us to consolidate cargo from different suppliers at the port of arrival.

The leading port candidates were all situated along the Black Sea or the Baltic Sea. I followed up on this conclusion with several phone calls to our suppliers to pinpoint the ports to which they had regular service. Once those ports were identified, I went on the hunt for a reliable provider who could handle the onward logistics to Bishkek.

In the end, the search was narrowed down to two viable routes. The first, favored by exporters of Turkish citruses to Central Asia, went through the port city of Novorossiysk, Russia, situated along the Black Sea. The route was longer than the one offered by nearby Poti, but it was faster since it involved just two border crossings, through Russia and Kazakhstan. The problem with Novorossiysk, however, was that none of our poultry suppliers operated any traffic through there.

The second option was the port of Klaipeda, Lithuania. Klaipeda was situated along the Baltic Sea and proved an ideal candidate: not only was it faster, but Sadia and Tyson had regular deliveries there, enabling us to consolidate the required 160 tons of mostly Bush legs, chicken broilers, and frankfurters. As such, Klaipeda offered us a logistical edge that the competing ports along the Baltic Sea— including those in St. Petersburg, Russia and Riga, Latvia—could not. We had a winner.

It was several days later, as I was working out the final touches to our new supply route, when Nahas walked into my office.

Fig. 4 Map showing different rail routes to Bishkek, Kyrgyzstan.

"What's this?" he asked, staring at my scribbles on the map.

"It looks like we're going to start using Klaipeda for Kyrgyzstan," I said, readying to walk him through the new route.

"That's great, but we won't be needing it for long."

"Excuse me? Are we backing out of Central Asia now?" I could not bear the thought, especially that I now saw we had a real fighting chance.

"Nope, we're not backing out. But soon, we're going to start using zeppelins for deliveries," he replied. "I will be investing in a startup that aims to revive the zeppelin. No more border crossings, no more ferry boats. Just a ten-day flight from Poti direct. We do our own scheduling, and the capacity is a manageable 40 tons per journey. You know what that means."

"Bananas?"

"Exactly, the journey is short enough for fresh bananas. And the best part?" He smiled. "I will personally be on that maiden voyage."

It was a fantastic solution to a logistical nightmare, one that held the promise of revolutionizing the way we did business in Central Asia—but, unfortunately, it was too far-fetched. Trust in the zeppelin had never recovered in the wake of widespread images of the Hindenburg disaster of 1937, which showed a passenger-laden airship suspended in midair erupting in flames. Besides, flying a zeppelin above the *stan* republics was bound to raise several questions related to security and espionage. The revival of the zeppelin was a cute idea, one that Nahas would toy with for years—but it would never come to fruition.

By July of that year, the good news started trickling in. The changes introduced to the supply and demand sides of our operation were coming together nicely like pieces of a puzzle. I heard from our logistics providers that our first shipment of frozen poultry products had just arrived at our warehouse in Bishkek, which lay along the path of the railway track. An expectant, newly expanded distribution platform was meanwhile readying to fire on all cylinders. But when I got in touch with Smayra to inquire about how the discharge operation was going, I learned of a serious and unexpected development.

"There is no train," Smayra said.

"What do you mean there is no train?" I asked in alarm. "The logistics company says that the goods arrived and are being discharged as we speak! Did you get in touch with our team at the warehouse?"

"I'm at the warehouse myself, and I'm telling you, there is no train here."

We were now on the receiving end of another reality check. There was simply nothing straightforward about conducting business in these parts. Our wagons, they had vanished.

It took 24 hours of non-stop investigative work before Smayra finally located the wagons, which had diverted to discharge our goods at a competitor's warehouse. It was daylight burglary, but a situation that Smayra managed to resolve after escalating the matter through his connections in Bishkek.

Once our goods were finally recuperated and the hiccup was cleared, Smayra and his team managed to distribute 15 tons of frozen chicken meat in the first two days of activity. It was more than he had previously managed in a month prior to expanding our distribution network. Just like that, he was on the comeback trail, shaking off the Van Cleef moniker to reclaim Tom Jones status.

The following year, I made another trip to Bishkek. I happened to be there on the 8th of March—International Women's Day—the most anticipated bank holiday on the nation's calendar. Smayra, relishing his newfound success, was celebrating the accomplishments of our company in Kyrgyzstan, which took after a popular woman's name: Stella Foods. To mark the occasion, he concocted a special brew of herbs and spices from his private garden, which—sitting on his terrace—we enjoyed with Hank Mobley's *The Turnaround!* playing in the background. We later made our way to Navigator for a celebratory round of White Russian cocktails. Smayra, grinning at the sight of our raised drinks, declared, "These glasses look a lot more than half-full to me!" From that point onward, the White Russian would become my beverage of choice.

CHAPTER NINETEEN
A CASE OF PRIVATIZATION ON STEROIDS IN ROMANIA

In the winter of 2000, I stood at the Piața Operei in the center of Timișoara, Romania. I had just completed the drive from Cluj-Napoca, located in Count Dracula's Transylvania region, as part of a broader tour of our distribution network in the country. It was a particularly harsh winter that year, and I was having to endure lows of -20 degrees Celsius at every stop north of the country's Apuseni Mountains. *Welcome to the world of a frozen chicken,* I thought.

The purpose of my trip, my second in three months, was to inspect our fulfilment centers scattered around Romania. We had a presence in the capital Bucharest, Constanța, Bacău, Iași and Cluj-Napoca, as well as where I now stood—in Timișoara. In each of those locations, we operated central cold stores and a string of reefer containers to store and handle fruit. The ability to especially ripen bananas locally in every major city enabled us to reach a wider customer base and to improve our order fulfillment capability. (At the time, Romania imposed a prohibitive $835 tariff for every ton of imported poultry meat. This amounted to as much as 250 percent of the cost of the product itself—depending on the part—and discouraged us from distributing poultry products in the country.)

The square I was standing in now was the birthplace of a bloody revolution eleven years earlier. The spontaneous uprising culminated in the dramatic show-trial and execution of the head of Romania's Communist party, President Nicolae Ceaușescu, and his wife, Elena. The revolution marked the end of 42 years of Communist rule and set Romania on a sure footing toward European Union membership—heralding a new dawn of radical political, social, and economic reform. It was the beginning of the end for poverty and corruption in the country, two maladies that had plagued the local populace for decades.

Despite an air of optimism, however, the pace of reforms was sluggish. Romania's economy remained frail and poverty was pervasive—particularly outside the capital—even after 11 years had passed since the revolution. Legacy Stalinist architecture dominated every residential, commercial, and industrial quarter, while Trabant vehicles—once the pride of the Eastern Bloc—still littered the streets, serving as eerie demonstrations of communism's stubborn hold on everyday life.

Still, the legislative foundations for institutional reforms had been laid, and Romania was inching toward full compliance with European Union membership guidelines. Conforming to those guidelines would also unlock much-needed loans from the IMF and the World Bank designed to modernize the economy.

While the Romanian market held promise, very little was forthcoming via foreign direct investments. Opportunities to participate in the economy's transformation were plentiful and could be pursued through investments in commerce and industry. Though those remained risky and complicated endeavors, they held the prospect of attractive returns for trailblazers daring to engage in early days. For our organization, the proposition to be among the pioneers in the Romanian market was not only appealing. It was also perfectly aligned with our broader aspirations for the region. In fact, it was the country's geographic situation and our ambitions for the markets neighboring the Black Sea that justified the expansion of our supply lines to Romania in the first place.

Romania sits along Europe's eastern border limit. It would be completely landlocked if not for a narrow coastal strip granting the country access to a seaport along the Black Sea—the Port of Constanța. The port provides direct access for internationally shipped product, including bananas, to enter the country. Additionally, Romania's coastline hosts the delta of the Danube River (Europe's second largest waterway, after the Volga), providing a path for intermodal transshipments on their way from the Black Sea to Central Europe. The completion of the Danube-Black Sea Canal in 1987, linking the river with the port, earned Constanța prominence as an important logistical hub.

There was one drawback to the port being situated along the Black Sea: any sea journey from the high seas to Constanța necessitated costly and time-consuming passages through the straits of the Dardanelles and the Bosporus. A banana shipment as ours, sailing from the port of Guayaquil, Ecuador, was additionally having to navigate through the Panama Canal and the Strait of Gibraltar, making for a very expensive voyage. But even this drawback played to our advantage as operators in nearby Turkey and the Caucasus. For such a journey to make financial sense, the accumulated shipping costs had to be spread over a volume of bananas significantly larger than that which the Romanian market could accommodate. Because we had service to nearby ports in Poti, Gemlik and Mersin, we could piggyback our deliveries to Romania on the same vessels. In this way, we exploited logistical synergies for all our markets in the region.

In addition to optimizing on shipping costs, our unique region-wide presence gave us a tremendous advantage when managing relationships with suppliers. Despite their being significantly larger and more powerful than us, global brands came to depend on us as A-list distributors the same way that we relied on them for the security of vital supply lines.

Thus, our footprint in the countries surrounding the Black Sea provided an edge to our supply chain in Romania, although this alone, we knew, would not guarantee us success. To complement that advantage, we invested heavily in cutting-edge fruit ripening facilities and technologies. We also allocated a sizable investment toward widening the breadth of our distribution network, which came to span every corner of the country.

Leveraging our good standing with Dole, we also acquired the rights to distribute Cavendish bananas in the Republic of Moldova, a smaller landlocked country to the northeast of Romania. Our partner there, Vladimir Sula, was an unlikely entrepreneur who started his journey operating a supermarket in the capital, Chişinău. Sula would source bananas from our bonded warehouses in Constanţa to sell at his supermarket before venturing into distribution. His loyalty and work ethic eventually convinced us to broaden the scope of our relationship, and an investment was poured into a state-of-the-art cold store in Chişinău. Sula's product portfolio only grew from there; soon he was distributing Sadia products and Jan-Peter Schøpp's Atlantic mackerel, in addition to Dole bananas. Moldova would become a full-fledged operation.

Sula was a taciturn man who spoke only when necessary. When he smiled, he flashed a set of prosthetic gold teeth that doubled as a status symbol. I often visited him at his supermarket, where his offices were also located. Violence in Moldova was not uncommon, and as a precautionary measure, Sula arranged his desk so that it faced the door. A wall behind him separated the compound from the parking lot outside. A narrow window was fitted close to the ceiling, providing privacy to the outside world behind him. He was a man of modest physical stature, and when he sat, the back frame of his swivel chair towered over his head and shoulders.

As it turned out, even this cautious arrangement was not bullet-proof—or shall I say, bomb-proof. One morning, the phone on Sula's desk rang. Upon picking up, an explosive device planted by a competitor on the windowsill behind him went off. Miraculously, he survived this attempt on his life, saved by the frame of his chair and an emergency airlift to Bucharest for treatment. A few weeks later, the scars and burns still not completely healed, Sula was back at his desk.

A few months after the incident, Sula and I were driving from Chişinău into Iaşi, across the Romanian border, when I asked what had motivated him to carry on after the assassination attempt.

"You have to carry on," he said.

But while he did *carry on*, he had certainly done so in a more cautious manner. In the aftermath of the explosion, Sula rearranged his office so that his desk was now away from the window. His gold dental prosthetics were replaced with white porcelain—an attempt at lowering his profile, or perhaps, a subtle sign of an evolving landscape as an entire region pressed forward in its quest for modernity.

One thing became abundantly clear, however. Much as Sula intended to return to normalcy, violence is detrimental for business, especially when one is at the receiving end. The brazen murder attempt spooked suppliers and customers alike, resulting in a lingering drop in business.

Beyond bananas, our experience in Romania reaffirmed the notion that opportunities tend to present themselves only *after* one enters the game. Certainly, there was money in distribution, which we earned by leading the market on supply reliability, product quality, and logistical breadth. But the truly exceptional wins were realized through the acquisition of formerly state-owned assets that went on the market at highly discounted prices.

To understand how those opportunities came along requires a familiarity with events that unfolded in the '90s—a time that saw Romania pursue reforms to its political, social, and economic landscapes. It was the age of Mass Privatization Programs, begun a decade earlier with the transfer of state-owned assets to private citizens across Central Europe, and now reaching Eastern Europe and the former states of the Soviet Union. This tidal wave of market liberalization finally swept into Romania in 1992, lagging three years behind the change in political system triggered by the fall of Ceaușescu's totalitarian regime.

At the heart of any privatization program is the transfer of state-owned companies, including those with activities in infrastructure and industry, to private entities. The intended aim is the creation of a broad social class of capitalists that could govern businesses more efficiently than a centralized government apparat would. There were different methodologies for going about a privatization program. Various European countries had already experimented with several, offering Romania a plethora of precedents to draw lessons from. Of those, four stood out: the direct sale of assets to the highest bidder, employee buyouts, the restitution of assets to their previous owners and the issuance of equal-access vouchers.

Each of these approaches was characterized by distinct advantages and drawbacks. The direct sale of assets, for instance, guaranteed the highest revenues to government, but was slow to roll out. It also compromised fairness. Employee buyouts, on the other hand, handed over assets to industry specialists who already understood the business, but they deprived those assets of any real chance of a fresh capital injection. The restitution of assets to their original (pre-Communist Era) owners served to restore confidence in property ownership rights—but this process, too, was often lengthy and fraught with endless disputes.

In Romania, time and fairness were identified as the national priorities for the program. The government consequently pursued the equal-access voucher track (following in the footsteps of Russia and Poland), which was fast and fair by design. Pursuant to this methodology, vouchers—essentially ownership certificates—were distributed to citizens, who could in turn freely trade each for a share in a government-owned asset of their choice.

Romania began to roll out the program in 1992. Initially, it was hampered by the reluctance of government officials to cede control of assets; to do so was to relinquish power. In fact, 70 percent of assets remained in the hands of the state even three years after the rollout of the program had begun, hindering any real socioeconomic progress. This procrastination eventually invited more pressure from the EU—which Romania had applied to join—as well as from lenders, such as the IMF and the World Bank. In the end, the government yielded. A second, more serious drive was made in 1995 to accelerate the program through the enactment of robust and binding changes to the original privatization laws.

The voucher system Romania opted for was not without its flaws, of course. Chief among those was the resultant fragmented ownership of assets. Single entities came to be held by thousands of individuals—none of which had any real control over them. This curtailed the ability to implement any effective mechanisms for governance and decision-making.

As it were, the shortcomings of the equal-access voucher methodology far outweighed its merits. Once vouchers were in the hands of the masses, it crystalized that they would be of no real value to anyone. Additionally, the cash-strapped populace who came to own these minority shares had very limited access to the investment funds and expertise required to modernize the assets, especially in the absence of foreign direct investments. Many became disillusioned with the scheme and resorted to selling their shares at discounts nearing 90 percent of the face value.

Over the next couple of years, intermediary Investment Privatization Funds came to the rescue, operating as vehicles that consolidated representation of individual voucher-holders. These privatization funds traded blocks of vouchers for majority ownership and management rights in specific assets on behalf of their clients. This resolved the fragmented ownership problem, and it was now possible to centralize governance over any one asset—a prerequisite to effective management.

By the turn of the millennium, the value of assets run by these privatization funds finally began to appreciate. Many of the original voucher owners were eager to profit and pressured the funds to offload assets to private investors. The subsequent listing of assets on the market far exceeded investor appetite, however, despite a sevenfold increase in foreign direct investment in the country over that period. While the original voucher owners still profited, the disparity in supply and demand led to auctioning off assets at bargain prices.

Our group stood among the few outfits with the appetite to invest in Romania at the time. There were several incentives for doing so, not the least of which were the weakening of the national currency against the dollar and a high inflation rate, both of which strengthened our hand as we submitted our offers.

We proceeded to make a winning bid for the logistics hub we had been renting for storage and handling in Ploeşti (on the outskirts of Bucharest). We also acquired reefer storage space at the port of Constanţa, along with the rights to operate the adjacent pier—a key logistical link in our supply chain. Finally, we took control of all 120 reefer rail wagons that crisscrossed the country carrying our bananas and other refrigerated items. Every acquisition was a triumph for us and a triumph for Romania, as it brought about the creation of jobs, the proliferation of expertise and the influx of hard currency.

Over the next seven years, Romania witnessed a property bubble that saw realty prices, including those we had acquired, grow tenfold. They say timing is everything. To be a pioneer—braving the risks to be the first at the scene—is to perfect that timing.

CHAPTER TWENTY
FROM RUSSIA, WITH LOVE

As we reaped the rewards of our ventures in Romania and Moldova, we were gearing for another boon in the Caucasus in 2004. The region was set on an upward trajectory, buoyed by government reforms and the progress made on the Baku-Tbilisi-Ceyhan pipeline—which was now nearing completion. Market sentiment was bullish, and consumption trends were evolving in sophistication. For one, demand was markedly shifting away from cheap leg-quarter protein and toward whole chicken and further processed products. We were well-positioned to cater to this new form of demand—and indeed championed it—through our growing joint venture with Sadia.

But a wider product portfolio and exponential growth made for an increasingly complex scope for our supply operation to contend with. This presented us with several challenges, including a strained capacity for order fulfillment and a growing cashflow constraint.

First, the ability to fulfill orders perfectly was a vital indicator of our supply stream's health. Among other things, it reflected the extent to which our orders were packaged and shipped in full and delivered on time. To execute a perfect order, there can be no room for error at any stage of the supply chain, which, for our venture with Sadia, stretched from the farms in Brazil to our points of sales dotting the Silk Road.

With demand suddenly diversified to include dozens of new items, we struggled to meet the order fulfilment targets we had set ourselves. Many of the shipments we received were now carrying the wrong items, often product that we found difficult to sell and would stack up at our warehouses for months. Even then, many deliveries were failing to reach our warehouses in a timely manner, incurring demurrages and other unnecessary fees along the way. The blame was tossed back and forth among the vested parties of our operation and the issue eventually became politicized, making it harder to identify the root cause of our collective shortcomings. In the meantime, profitability suffered, complicating our relationship with Sadia.

Dr. Motta, who held a senior executive role at Sadia, remained the biggest proponent of our joint venture, having helped set it up. Now in his sixties, he had established his bona fides by introducing Sadia chicken to the world. His successes over the preceding 30 years had given him an aura of invincibility at Sadia. But on his journey to the top, Dr. Motta had ruffled a few feathers beyond the chicken coop. Not everyone shared in his upbeat sentiment toward our joint venture, which had grown to span countries across the Caucasus, Central Asia, and Eastern Europe.

I was on a call with Dr. Motta, brainstorming ideas to get our supply streams to catch up with the growing, ever-diversified demand. We soon realized that we lacked sufficiently clean and consolidated data and the visibility required to drill down to the source of our supply issues. Without that clarity, we could not hope to overcome our challenges. If, on the other hand, we could establish the facts, then the underlying causes could be clearly defined, and we would already be halfway toward a solution.

In the end, I put forward a suggestion. "The *M/V Arctic Wolf* is set for loading later this February. Why don't I tail her cargo on the ground as it flows from one end of the supply stream to the other? We'll see if anything stands out."

"That is a great idea. I can arrange for you to be at our fulfillment centers, and then again at the loading port in Itajaí, Brazil."

"And once the vessel arrives in Poti the following month, I can liaise with Asly to secure access to the port and our warehouses at Poti and Tbilisi. We would then have all the data we need to compare what was ordered, shipped, and received at different stages of the supply chain."

Almost immediately after the call, I set off to the state of Santa Catarina in Brazil, where Sadia ran the bulk of their operations, to trail the cargo allocated for loading aboard the *M/V Arctic Wolf.* Being on the ground provided me with the opportunity to converse with people across different functions, including production, scheduling, shipping, and fulfillment. The main issue behind our short shipments stood out almost immediately and had its roots in communication—or rather the lack of it.

When a requested item such as the fast-selling 1 kg chicken griller was not available for fulfillment, those in charge of dispatch would replace it with a substitute, which could be a 1.5 kg chicken griller, or a 1 kg chicken griller packaged under one of Sadia's less recognized brands. The dispatchers did this in good faith, ignorant of the fact that local consumer preferences often made those substitutes an extremely difficult sell. Furthermore, the dispatchers had no open communication channels with us and often had to make these decisions operating in silos.

There was a quick fix to this problem: the establishment of communication channels with key individuals at Itajaí's fulfilment centers. This helped streamline priorities and the allocation of replacement items when a specific request for an item could not be met. We also agreed on *if/then rules* that could be followed to automate decision-making on the spot.

Once product arrived in Georgia, another problem appeared that was of a more sinister nature. A significant percentage of the product that left the processing facilities in Brazil never made it to our warehouses here. Our working hypothesis was that there was theft, and that it was happening during the discharge operation at the port of Poti.

The following month, the *M/V Arctic Wolf* arrived in the Black Sea on schedule. I flew to Tbilisi and made the commute by car to Poti, reviewing my notes along the way—including those taken aboard the *M/V Bolivar* in Mersin earlier—to remind myself of the antics deployed by gangs of longshoremen and others to skim cargo at the ports: boxes thrown overboard, clothing modified with large hidden pockets, ballasts on trucks, and so on. But even as I thought it through, the numbers did not add up. The volume of product we were losing with every shipment in Poti was almost three times higher than what was typical at any other port. Just then, a cow appeared to be crossing our road up ahead, interrupting my thoughts—but the driver made no attempt to slow down or steer the car. "Careful!" I screamed.

He laughed. "Don't worry. When a cow walks, it never changes direction. There is no risk."

But I knew all too well about the risks of being on the road in Georgia at the time. The near miss served as a reminder of what could await me.

At the port in Poti, everything was in place to commence the discharge operation. Reefer rail wagons and trucks were in position, as were longshoremen, crane operators, and forklift drivers. I was standing aboard the *M/V Arctic Wolf*'s deck again, reunited with her crew, as a customs officer broke the hatch seals to set the operation in motion. Like the rest of our arrivals, the cargo was loaded in loose break bulk cases, increasing the risk of embezzlement. I was adamant not to leave the port until the ship had emptied its haul—which was expected to take 2 to 3 days—and was set to sail out to sea again.

On the first day of operations, there was nothing to raise any eyebrows. The trucks appeared to come and go with no sign of ballast jettison. Furthermore, the trucks returning from the port to our warehouses were unloading quantities that matched the exact figures displayed on their manifests—suggesting no cargo was being lost to the road. At night, I combed the ship's starboard side over and over, but nothing was thrown overboard.

The second day also passed without anything worthy of note. Perhaps, I thought to myself, *my mere presence here was deterring any suspicious behavior.* By then, however, several of the ship's hatches had been completely emptied, which enabled me to compare the numbers shown on the ship's manifest with what had already arrived at our cold stores. The exercise led to the shocking discovery that a significant quantity of product had disappeared right under my nose. It was a vanishing act that made David Copperfield look like a schoolboy. I was perplexed.

I spent that night on the *M/V Arctic Wolf*'s deck lying on my back, looking up at the starry night and listening to Pink Floyd's *Shine On You Crazy Diamond.* On my mind was one question: how was that cargo disappearing?

On the third and final day of the discharge, I decided to step off deck and onto the berthing area for a change of perspective. I stood beside one of the trailers as an investigator would, watching cargo being winched down, tallied, and loaded onto a trailer. Once the trailer was fully loaded, its content was captured on the manifest, and a seal with a unique serial number was fixed to the doors as a measure of control to deter tampering with the cargo as it transited to the warehouse.

With the trailer readying to drive off, something extraordinary caught my eye—something I had not seen at any other port. The bolts holding the trailer's container doors together looked as though they had been tampered with. The paint job exhibited scratch marks consistent with the rotating motion of a wrench. To avoid breaking any seals, I figured, drivers were unbolting the heavy doors off containers altogether.

There was still one loose end to the mystery: the quantities discharged at the warehouse had matched what was on the manifests. The missing product could only be explained if the quantity originally loaded onto a trailer exceeded that stated on the manifest—the difference earmarked for theft. For that to happen, the tallyman and the customs officer with the seals had to be in on the truck driver's act, implying a highly organized crime. There was no other way.

I hurriedly called Asly in Tbilisi and told him about the discovery. As he listened intently, I suggested that we stop one of the sealed trailers before it left the port. We would unload it and match the content with what was on the manifest. If the quantity were surplus, that would confirm my suspicion.

"I have a better idea," he said. "We'll ask several loaded trailers to wait at the port, then provide an armed convoy to escort them to the warehouse. These guys can be dangerous, it would be better to open the containers at our warehouse where we have control over security. In the meantime, I suggest you get out of there immediately."

Within an hour, I was on my way driving west toward Trabzon, Turkey, which was almost equidistant to Tbilisi. From there, I would catch an internal flight back to Istanbul. Asly, meanwhile, arranged for the convoy. As suspected, the trailers were found to be overloaded with cargo that was set to be offloaded somewhere along the journey to our warehouses.

A few days later, I heard from Asly that our offices in Poti were torched in a suspected retaliatory act. The uncovering of the port scam had cost the colluders a sizable source of revenue.

"Don't lose sleep over it. No one was hurt," Asly said pragmatically, "the furniture we lost is worth a lot less than the tens of thousands of dollars we were losing with every shipment."

After supply and fulfilment accuracy, the second challenge we faced because of our rapid growth was that related to cashflow. Larger sales volumes required pouring more working capital into the operation. Because we operated a joint venture with Sadia, the increased exposure would impact both sides.

Accordingly, the string of security incidents we suffered primarily in Georgia, Azerbaijan and Moldova had rattled Sadia as they weighed the benefits of our venture against the risk exposure to their investment in the region. Our tolerance to risk was clearly higher than theirs—as a listed company, they were curtailed by stricter corporate governance rules and regulations. Despite an air of optimism from having resolved the supply-related issues at Itajaí and Poti, the heightened risks hinted at a chasm within Sadia's boardroom that was threatening the future of our partnership.

In the end, Dr. Motta came through for us, leveraging his

influence to grant a lifeline to our joint venture. The Value at Risk, a complex calculation of the total financial exposure brought about by the operation, was capped at a level that Sadia was comfortable with. Things returned to normal.

But that normal did not last long. A few months later, in September 2004, I was at Istanbul when I received a distress call from Dr. Motta.

"The Ministry of Agriculture in Russia has just banned the import of Brazilian meat products alleging foot-and-mouth disease," he said.

I knew that Sadia had a major presence in Russia and would be drastically affected by such a ban.

"We have a consignment aboard the *M/V Nova Zembla* that has already sailed for St. Petersburg, Russia. She needs to be diverted immediately," he continued, before adding, "we have a clean bill of health for the product, but it is all labeled in Russian—which means our only option is to divert the vessel to Poti." Dr. Motta was right. Georgia, Azerbaijan, and Armenia, which were accessible through Poti, all accepted Russian-packaged goods since the language was still widely spoken there. But the volume of product on board was several times that of our regular service and would be problematic for us to distribute profitably.

"I completely understand the bind you are in," I replied, "but it would probably take us six months before we could move that kind of volume. If we agree to take on this product, the disruption to our operation and our cashflow would be enormous!" My stated position was sincere, rather than a tactic to gain positional advantage. Yet we owed a huge debt to Dr. Motta, who had stood by us when our relationship with Sadia had soured earlier.

"Listen, you set the price. You set the payment terms. Besides, if you grant us this favor, certain figures are bound to see the strategic value of your operation to Sadia."

"This is a big call to make. Give me a couple of hours to discuss things internally," I said.

Following a three-way call with Nahas and Asly, we unanimously agreed to receive the cargo aboard the *M/V Nova Zembla*. The size of the consignment made it considerably larger than what we could comfortably chew. But we considered the decision an investment of sorts in our relationship with Sadia, rather than as a play for financial profitability, which it was not expected to be.

The following week, Nahas and I happened to be in Milan for a scheduled meeting with Dr. Motta and his team. Dr. Motta liked to spoil himself and those around him. As the quintessential Milanese boulevardier, he deemed it necessary to host Nahas and me over a fine seven-course meal at *Il Luogo di Aimo e Nadia*, a Michelin 2-star restaurant on the outskirts of the city.

At the restaurant, we were duly asked to leave our mobile phones at the concierge desk before being shown to our table. I could tell that all was not well with Dr. Motta. He looked uncharacteristically edgy and was taking it out on our increasingly embarrassed sommelier. Dr. Motta had already sent back two expensive wine bottles—not because there was anything wrong with the wine, but because he was not satisfied with how they paired with our hors d'oeuvre and appetizer.

From there, however, the soirée progressed a little more smoothly, and by the time our main course was served, Dr. Motta was back to his joyous self again, only to be interrupted—mid-quail—by the concierge.

"There is an urgent call on your mobile," the lady whispered.

Dr. Motta took the call and returned to the table a few short minutes later, a vigorous blood-rush to his head eclipsing his trademark Mediterranean tan.

"The *M/V Nova Zembla* was a blunder," he said, looking like a chess player about to knock over his king in resignation. When Sadia reissued the invoices for the cargo diverted from Russia to Poti, the Value at Risk indicator monitored by Dr. Motta's opponents at Sadia had jumped three-fold, sending alarm bells singing. The issue escalated rapidly, and we now found ourselves on the verge of being penalized for an act intended as a goodwill gesture.

It was obvious to everyone that our time as Sadia's partners in the region was coming to an end, even as Nahas, seated next to me, struggled to come to terms with the setback.

"Why?!" he finally burst out loud, to the horror of the proud patrons of *Il Luogo di Aimo e Nadia*. "Tyson, Dole, Chiquita, and my mother all say that we are the best!"

EPILOGUE

In August of 2005, I was back at Istanbul's Bayrampaşa Hali, sipping tea from a Turkish tea glass. I was on the phone trying to resolve an issue with the *M/V Santiago Star*, resting at the anchorage zone reserved for the port in Mersin. The vessel's berthing instructions had been expected a day earlier when a tugboat would have pulled her to the quay to drop a heavy load of bananas. As it happened, the port's two tugboats were temporarily placed out of service because of technical failures, and our agents were left to invest all their experience, connections, and emotions in scouring for an alternative. Distress calls were made to every port and harbor within 200 nautical miles of Mersin—including Iskenderun, Limassol, and a moonshot to Beirut.

In the greater scheme of things, the delay was a fleeting logistical hiccup, hardly worthy of note. A setback like this is not completely unexpected even at the world's most advanced ports. The truth was that our operation in Mersin had witnessed remarkable progress since the discharge of the *M/V Bolivar* in 1999. It had evolved to become the crown jewel of our portfolio of ventures. In addition to a fruit handling facility, a packing house, and a reefer trucking company, we operated bonded cold stores inside Mersin Serbest Bölgesi—the area designated a free zone at the port—from which we catered to exports and other cargo transiting through Turkey.

It had taken a remarkable collective effort to arrive at where we were. Along that journey, we overcame many of the same hurdles that we were still facing elsewhere along the Silk Road—trade wars, vague regulation, inadequate infrastructure—but we were now reaping the fruits of the long game. Furthermore, Mersin provided a proven blueprint that we could emulate at our other locations.

Indeed, we met with comparable achievements elsewhere. We built several successful ventures from the ground up, securing supply lines, expanding our distribution infrastructure—that was at the cutting-edge—and diversifying our offering. Our integrated cold chain in Romania was thriving, as were our distribution networks across Turkey, Georgia, and Moldova.

But we also suffered our fair share of disappointments. One was our inability to sustain our presence in Azerbaijan, despite several years of profitable growth; another was our below-par success in Armenia, where we failed to capitalize on the potential of our first-mover advantage. In other places yet, we huffed and puffed but failed to blow the door down. Such was the case in Turkmenistan and Uzbekistan, which remained mostly off-limits to foreign investors.

On the road, we grew. I grew. My interactions with the people I met along the way—from the chicken catchers in Chapecó to the longshoremen at the port of Poti—were what made the journey worthwhile. Sharing in the local cultures, especially along the Silk Road, was what enriched it. I strove to leave my mark any place I went, countering turbulence with dynamism. Yet I upheld one constant in the face of it all: my ideals.

Now, I was nearing the end of my journey along the Silk Road. It was a journey that lived up to its promise in every way. But rather than quench my thirst for the romantic route, it left me yearning for more. Upon exiting the region, I would hop aboard another trade caravan that took me deep into sub-Saharan Africa, where I would start a new and equally exhilarating existence from my new base in Conakry, Guinea. (That is a tale for another day.)

My decision to depart corresponded with a time of renewal for many of the members on our team. Some, like Nahas and Sidani, had grown their initial investment sufficiently and were looking to cash in their chips. Others, like Chalabi in Azerbaijan, Smayra in Kyrgyzstan, and Baron Khachig and Wehbe in Armenia, were on their last stint and would soon retire. Aoun, who was offered a lease extension on his life following his abduction ordeal, opted for repatriation and a fresh start at home. There were also those who opted to stay behind; Asly and indeed Sakalaki and Bekai would become Silk Road lifers, forever enchanted and unable to escape the region's allure. They would reinvent themselves in the industry and continue to operate independently.

Our successes, when and where registered, came not without hardship. The nature of our work was demanding, particularly dealing with bananas and other perishable products; travel to and within our markets was seldom straightforward, be it by plane, train, or automobile; destinations were often harsh, especially at the ports and bazaars. There were times when we fell and merely scratched our knees. There were times when we contended with macabre scenarios, culminating in the desperately low points of a murder, a kidnapping, and a targeted bombing.

That day at the *hal*, I allowed myself a moment of reflection. I could not let the question escape me, as I weighed the rewards of my journey against the hardships. *Was the journey worth it?*

Given the choice, I would take the good, leaving the ugly behind. But life does not happen that way. It is hard to consider a life well-lived in the absence of progress, and there is very little progress to be made in the absence of risk. In the end, it is the journey that we choose—our collective experience—that defines us. *So, was it all worth it?*

On a personal level, the response to that question is terribly deep and personal, influenced by childhood experiences, personal values, even insecurities. It is further shaped by my role models and my outlook on life. Above all, it is fueled by an intrinsic craving for adventure.

When examined from a purely business perspective, the answer is simpler and pertains to the elementary calculus that ties opportunity with risk and reward. Beyond a certain risk threshold, however, an X factor is required to keep the faith. That X factor is optimism, the form based on tangible capabilities. This holds especially true when operating in emerging markets—at once dynamic, vague, and unpredictable—which tend to give up their secrets only long after the initial commitment of time and money had been made.

As I pondered the question, my reflective state was disturbed by a sudden ruckus near the entrance to our outlet No. 57 at the *hal*. I set down my tea glass on a stack of banana cases and walked over to the scene of the commotion to find a roaring gang of fruit peddlers. At the center of the gathering stood an impeccably dressed young intern receiving the finishing touches of a shoeshine. I stared deep into his innocent eyes. *Absolutely.* I said to myself. *This journey was worth it.* I turned my attention to the shoeshine man. *"Hadi abi, ekstra baharatlı yap,"* I said with a wry smile, suggesting he make the impending serving of chili pepper especially hot.

With that, I walked back to my tea glass and made another call—hoping for an update on the berthing of the *M/V Santiago Star* in Mersin.

APPENDIX A: THE LESSONS

Today, I look back to my years on the Silk Road with the lucidity afforded by the monocle of retrospect. I revive and celebrate the lessons acquired along that journey with much fondness. That chapter in my life would lack due closure if I were not to impart those lessons in the hope that they may be of value to others. I shall therefore end these pages by sharing the wisdom I gained from a life in supply.

ON WINNING

Every venture is a triumph, regardless of the outcome. Search for fulfilment in the journey, and not at the finish line. After all, the journey is where we spend most of our lives, while the finish line is a place that we pass in one fleeting moment.

ON LOSING

A loss only qualifies as such when it yields irreparable physical or psychological trauma to those involved. Such a loss can be devastating, and we may have to learn to live with it for the rest of our lives. Every other type of loss is easily convertible to valuable experience points.

ON VALUES

Stay true to your values at all costs. We make tens of thousands of decisions each day; while most may be trivial, it is the sum of these decisions that dictates whether we succeed or fail in our higher endeavors. When we are driven by our values, we become confident and consistent in our decision-making, especially in times of doubt. We also ensure that our actions are aligned with our goals.

ON PRINCIPLES

Hold your principles in a perpetual state of work-in-progress, refining them as you grow in experience. Like values, principles serve to guide decision-making. But where values are rigid and set our standards, principles are malleable and provide us with a set of working rules.

ON MEANINGFUL EXPERIENCES

Rough seas make skillful sailors. Take the unbeaten track for a sure shot at an abundant and meaningful life. Think and act like a pioneer by adopting an adventurous mindset. Face adversity in the eye, it is hardship that will come to define us.

ON OPTIMISM

Informed optimism—founded on a tangible set of competencies, capabilities, and experiences—is a key ingredient for success. Blind optimism, that which draws on hope and faith alone, is a dangerous quality that can lead to ruin.

ON ORIENTATION

Strive to be a people person. You may have the best technology, processes, and assets at hand, but none of these can guarantee success in the absence of a motivated and competent team. Recognize that the most important investments are those made in hiring and developing the team. It is therefore essential for any venture to foster a people-centric culture as a foundation for quality and excellence. People are motivated by the prospect of being able to take control over their own lives. They will surprise you with their level of performance when given bigger responsibilities and provided with a strong culture of empowerment. Leverage local heroes, legend, and lore to reinforce such a culture.

ON GROWTH

Innovate...or vegetate. Have the courage to migrate to new technology early on, or risk falling behind. Be bold in your pursuit of change, even if it harms your interests in the short run. Ask lots of questions—curiosity killed the cat, but it also gave it nine lives. Push the envelope as far as you can and remember that no is only the start of the conversation.

ON TRAVEL

Be a local everywhere you go, travelling light on your own cultural luggage. The key to experiencing a foreign culture in a meaningful way is to think, talk, act, eat and, most importantly, drink as the locals do. This will earn you the love and respect of the locals and enrich your journey.

ON PERSONAL OBJECTIVES

Serve an idea that benefits the community or the environment first, and your personal interests second. Avoid personal goals that are purely financial, as those can blur your values and subsequent decision-making. If your purpose is of a noble nature, financial gains will present themselves as a natural byproduct. Show empathy and emphasize the *why*—not the *what*—when seeking to excite others. If you should find yourself unable to make a meaningful contribution to a situation, walk away.

ON COUNTING

Bake the pie first; worry about the size of your slice later. A precursor for success is the ability to recruit talent to support your cause. When setting out to achieve a goal, focus on onboarding the right people before worrying about how the spoils will be shared. A small slice of a large pie is more fulfilling than a large slice of no pie at all.

ON COMPETENCE

Develop a T-shaped skillset. The horizontal bar of the "T" represents a generalist skillset, broad but skin-deep. Being a generalist in this way improves your resilience in the face of disruption and enhances your ability to anticipate future events. The vertical part of the "T" suggests deep expertise in a narrow area, earning you an edge. By complementing your generalist skillset with specific subject matter expertise, you are set to benefit from the best of both worlds.

ON TIMING

Timing is everything. Acting on an opportunity too early or too late will impact the likelihood and extent of success. The good news is that timing is a competency that can be nurtured. First, develop the ability to read a situation so that you may better identify the right moment for action. Next, invest in your emotional intelligence so that you may acquire the discipline to act when that moment comes.

ON ASSERTIVENESS

Draw the line...on the line. It is important to mark your territory when you communicate. An invisible line separates your rights from the rights of other. Draw that line too close, and you invite others to encroach on what is yours. Draw it too far, and you become the aggressor. It is therefore imperative to demarcate the boundary at the point where your rights end and the rights of others begin. Doing so successfully makes you an assertive communicator who gets what is rightfully theirs every time—free of the burdens of guilt and conflict.

ON FREE MEALS

Beware the poisoned pawn, the seemingly innocent chess piece sacrificed for no apparent gain. For it is only after you have captured the pawn that a grander, more sinister, scheme is revealed, disadvantaging your position. There are no free meals on anyone's menu. Think twice before accepting one.

ON PARTNERSHIPS

There are invaluable advantages to be gained through collaborative partnerships. Choose to partner with those with whom you share common values, rather than common interests. Values are for life, while interests may change overnight. Success favors the longer-term view.

ON PROFESSIONAL NETWORKS

Insist on meaning in every business relationship. It is far more advantageous to count one or two industry leaders among your close associates than it is to have a nodding acquaintance with a broader patchwork of individuals. Cherish your valued relations and show them the loyalty they deserve, but condition that loyalty on the upholding of shared values.

ON SUPPLIER INFLUENCE

Shoot for symbiosis. Often, a key supplier will wield fantastic power that gives them the upper hand in the relationship. Do not submit to the status quo. Rather, seek to reengineer the value you contribute to the relationship so that you become an indispensable part of the supplier's value chain. Several levers may be at your disposal, such as providing a logistical service, innovating on a critical component, or investing in jointly owned infrastructure.

ON PURPOSE

Maintain singleness of purpose. Concentrating on a single idea enables you to focus finite resources, grow in competence, and, essentially, live your message. Have the courage to turn away distractions disguised as lofty business ideas. When you commit to an idea, commit fully, or do not commit at all.

ON SUPPLY STREAMS

Know the weakest link in your supply chain. Any chain is only as good as its weakest link, and a supply chain is no exception to that rule. To ensure the functional integrity of supply streams remains intact, maintain visibility over the flow of goods as they make their way from the earth—be it a farm, mine, well, or sea—to the final consumer.

ON NEGOTIATIONS

When engaged in a negotiation, avoid confusing your interests with your positions. Approach every negotiation as a problem to be overcome through the collaboration of the parties with a vested interest. Do not assume that different parties attach the same importance to each area of interest. When making or accepting concessions, ensure that the discourse remains fixed on those interests and allows for their relative importance to each party.

ON QUALITY

Never compromise on quality. An expensive, high-quality product is a superior proposition to a cheap, low-quality alternative. Achieving excellence in what you do requires airtight standards across the board, including those relating to people, suppliers, infrastructure, and processes.

ON MEASUREMENT

Measure your way to the treasure. As the adage goes, we cannot manage what we cannot measure. The ability to accurately measure input, process, and output parameters is a prerequisite for improving today's performance levels come tomorrow.

ON RISKS

With high risk comes the promise of high reward. Of course, the flip side is the prospect of a significant loss. When you encounter risk, meticulously plan for mitigative action to reap the associated rewards. To improve the chances of a favorable outcome, allocate generous time and money to building effective mitigation controls.

ON SUPPLY CONTINUITY

Supply continuity hinges on your ability to identify disruption at an early stage and on your robustness in dealing with adverse events. The ability to generate meaningful information from the length of the supply chain is the starting point for building such robustness. To do so, keep one eye on the farm and the other on the fork. Many organizations lack visibility beyond their immediate partners. They may be aware of the challenges faced by their own suppliers, but what about those confronting their second, third or fourth tier suppliers?

ON OPERATIONAL FLEXIBILITY

A flexible operation is one capable of rapidly adapting to changes in the market. A high degree of flexibility is desirable to ensure that the flow of supply can be increased, decreased, or even altered to keep up with changing demand patterns. To achieve this requires a degree of sophistication in network design and strategic thinking. Several avenues can be pursued to effect flexibility, including standardization, redundancies, and the decoupling of business activities.

ON SUPPLY EFFICIENCIES

Heed the need for speed. The velocity with which inventory passes through the supply chain has a direct impact on supply security, service quality, and ultimately, profitability. A higher velocity can and should be pursued by optimizing the supply network design, leveraging data analytics for decision-making, and adopting logistics-related technologies.

ON PRODUCT VARIETY

A wide product variety may suit your customers well, but it will also complicate your supply chain. For balance, restrict the scope of materials used upstream in the supply chain. This is possible by opting for versatile raw material that can be molded into hundreds or thousands of different items further down the chain.

ON PROFIT

Recognize that supply represents 50 percent of the profit equation. Many organizations fail to appreciate that there is as much to be gained on the sourcing front (supply) as there is on the sales front (demand). Many times, a profitable transaction is only possible when the buying price is right. It is therefore advisable to elevate your supply department to core-function status as a precursor to sustainable profitability.

ON REPUTATION

Guard your reputation with your life. A reputation, whether attached to a person or an organization, is a form of insurance that will get you up again should you get shot off your horse. Banks, investors, suppliers, customers, family, and friends are more likely to come through when your name carries goodwill. Reputations can be nourished through relationship and brand management and by fostering a mindset geared toward collaboration and innovation.

APPENDIX B: PHOTOGRAPHS

The *M/V Crown Sapphire* discharges her bounty of Dole bananas at the port of Gemlik, Turkey.

A *muzcu*, or banana peddler, carts produce through the streets of Samsun, Turkey.

Breakbulk bananas arrive at a reefer warehouse in Ploeşti, Romania.

A Trabant vehicle, once the pride of the Eastern Bloc, idles outside a cold store facility in Bacău, Romania.

Hardened men gather outside a flagship store at Dezerter Bazaar in Tbilisi, Georgia.

Sadia broilers are a permanent fixture at Georgia's bazaars.

A box of Chiquita bananas is acquired by a merchant for retail distribution in Tbilisi, Georgia.

The *M/V Nova Zembla*, carrying a heavy load of Tyson leg-quarters, docks at her designated berth in the port of Poti, Georgia.

Longshoremen load trucks and rail wagons with Tyson leg-quarters at the port of Poti for transit to Azerbaijan and Armenia.

An inflatable Dole banana graces a grocery storefront in Baku, Azerbaijan.

A solemn Republic Square captures the mood in Yerevan, Armenia.

Fresh fruits adorn the periphery of Central Market in Yerevan, Armenia.

Tyson leg-quarters thaw on display at a busy Osh Bazaar in Bishkek, Kyrgyzstan.

A single-screen cinema loops Bruce Lee's *Enter the Dragon* at Osh Bazaar in Bishkek, Kyrgyzstan.

A storekeeper readies his trusted abacus in Bishkek, Kyrgyzstan.

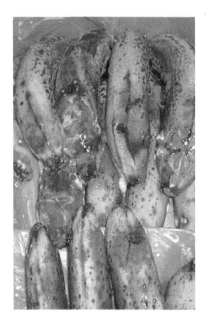

Unapologetic Cavendish bananas flaunt their fussy side.

ACKNOWLEDGEMENTS

Supply Unchained is a book that has been years in the making. It is a book about my early adventures in the world of supply. More importantly, it is a story about the people I met and interacted with along the way. It is the experiences that I shared with these people that provide the invaluable content for this book. Many of them are featured in the main pages of this book. Others have been spared mention but have left an equally indelible mark on my life. They include Fares Zouein, Roula Haddad, Cyril Rabbath, Fadi Ghanem, Roy Zirka, Reşat Ovalı, Rudy Ojail, Akram Nahas, Louise Cambaz, Habib Khoury, Jerry Alisson, Eric Joiner, Nadim Mamoun, Carlo Nicolo, Tamara Bokuchava, Pamela Bongiovanni, Fouad Foukra, Azad Bakersami, Gjert Myrestrand, and Antoine "Tintin" Massoud. I wish to wholeheartedly thank all of them for enriching my journey and broadening my worldview.

Capturing that journey in this book would not have been possible first and foremost without the support of my wife Raya, who provided encouragement, belief, and support at every hurdle. I am grateful for the endless wisdom she patiently offered as I bounced one idea after another off her. Her flair is palpable in every page. Thank you.

Thank you to my sister and fellow author Sara Ghannoum for her literary guidance and the hours and hours she invested in proof-reading this book. Any errors, grammatical or otherwise, are hers and hers alone.

The debt I owe to my editors, Janet Butler and William Hogeland, is enormous. I am grateful for their meticulous work, as well as for upholding the book's original spirit.

Thank you to Daniel Whitehead, whose insights and perspective have made this book a much more tolerable story.

Thank you to Candice Davidian Benmore for the exceptional creative work. Her perseverance toward finding common ground between her artistic vision for the book and my wanting opinions is commendable.

Thank you to Eleena Sarkissian and the team at Turning Point Books for the design and typography work. Also, their guidance at the publishing phase made all the difference.

A very warm and special thank you to Samih Ounsi for creating the maps included in this book. The narrative is lost without them.

BIBLIOGRAPHY

Alekberova, Fatma. "Impact of Armenia's Exclusion from Regional Energy Projects." *Turkish Asian Center for Strategic Studies*. 27 JUL 2012. https://tasam.org/Files/Icerik/File/impact_of_armenias_exclusion_from_regional_energy_projects_caf41ac2-9b5f-4d7a-9516-25cf27922b82.pdf.

Allen, Kristi. "Why China and America Fight over Chicken Feet." *Atlas Obscura*. January 28, 2019. https://www.atlasobscura.com/articles/chicken-feet-trade.

Asly, Fady. *Life with Scorpions: A Real Life Thriller*. 1st ed. Tbilisi: Mtsignobari, 2016.

Barkham, Patrick. "The Banana Wars Explained." *The Guardian*. March 05, 1999. https://www.theguardian.com/world/1999/mar/05/eu.wto3.

Castle, Stephen. "Pact Ends Long Trade Fight over Bananas." *The New York Times*. December 15, 2009. https://www.nytimes. com/2009/12/16/business/global/16banana.html.

"'Chicken Diplomacy' and Other Clinton-Yeltsin Campaign Scams Are Bad for Democracy, Bad for U.S. Taxpayers." *Center for Security Policy*. January 12, 2013. https://www. centerforsecuritypolicy.org/1996/03/28/chicken-diplomacy-and-other-clinton-yeltsin-campaign-scams-are-bad-for-democracy-bad-for-u-s-taxpayers-2/.

Depalma, Anthony. "Dole Says Trade Accord on Bananas Favors Rival." *The New York Times*. April 14, 2001. https://www.nytimes. com/2001/04/14/business/dole-says-trade-accord-on-bananas-favors-rival.html.

Depalma, Anthony. "U.S. and Europeans Agree on Deal to End hia." *The New York Times*. April 12, 2001. https://www.nytimes. com/2001/04/12/business/us-and-europeans-agree-on-deal-to-end-banana-trade-war.html.

Erlanger, Steven. "Chicken Parts and Politics on Agenda at Sinai Talks." *The New York Times*. March 28, 1996. https://www.nytimes. com/1996/03/28/world/chicken-parts-and-politics-on-agenda-at-sinai-talks.html.

"EU Defeat in Banana Export Battle." *BBC News*. August 01, 2005. http://news.bbc.co.uk/2/hi/business/4735983.stm.

"EU Suffers Defeat in Banana Wars." *BBC News.* April 07, 2008.
http://news.bbc.co.uk/2/hi/business/7335070.stm.

Food and Agriculture Organization of the United Nations.
Committee on Commodity Problems. *Intergovernmental Group
on Bananas and on Tropical Fruits.* Puerto De La Cruz: Ba/Tf 03/1,
2003.

Frisby, Michael K., and David Rogers. "Tamraz's White
House Access Intensifies Fund-Raising Charges." *The Wall
Street Journal.* March 17, 1997. https://www.wsj.com/articles/
SB858551963801120500.

Frisby, Michael K., and David Rogers. "White House-Tamraz Ties
Are Probed by Grand Jury." The Wall Street Journal. June 04, 1997.
https://www.wsj.com/articles/SB865389607126388000.

Fry, Jillian P., Nicholas A. Mailloux, David C. Love, Michael C.
Milli, and Ling Cao. *Feed Conversion Efficiency in Aquaculture:
Do We Measure It Correctly?* Bloomberg School of Public Health.
February 2018. https://jhu.pure.elsevier.com/en/publications/feed-
conversion-efficiency-in-aquaculture-do-we-measure-it-correc.

Gertz, Bill. "Clinton Vows Help for Yeltsin Campaign--Arkansas'
Interest in Poultry Dispute Discussed at Antiterrorism Summit."
The Washington Times, March 27, 1996.

Gertz, Bill. "Bill Clinton Leak Exposes Democrats' Double Standard on Impeachment." *The Washington Times*. December 10, 2019. https://www.washingtontimes.com/news/2019/dec/10/bill-clinton-boris-yeltsin-chicken-summit-exposes-/.

Gordon, Michael R. "International Business; U.S. Chickens in Russian Pots." *The New York Times*. January 18, 1996. https://archive.nytimes.com/query.nytimes.com/gst/fullpage-9900EFD611 39F93BA25752C0A960958260.html.

Greenberg, Paul. *Four Fish: The Future of the Last Wild Food*. New York: Penguin Books, 2011.

Gurbanov, Turab. *Le Pétrole de La Caspienne et La Politique Extérieure de L'Azerbaïdjan*. Paris: L'Harmattan, 2007.

Hatirli, Selim Adem, Eugene Jones, and Ali Rıza Aktaş. *Measuring the Market Power of the Banana Import Market in Turkey*. The Scientific and Technological Research Council of Turkey. Technical Paper No. 27 367-373, 2003. http://citeseerx.ist.psu.edu/viewdoc/download?doi=10.1.1.891.7581&rep=rep1&type=pdf.

Kraul, Chris. "Countries Split by International Banana Brouhaha. Plantations in Latin America Struggle to Survive under EU Import Quotas. United States Has Launched Probe." *Los Angeles Times*. August 03, 1995. https://www.latimes.com/archives/la-xpm-1995-08-03-fi-31044-story.html.

Levinson, Marc. *The Box: How the Shipping Container Made the World Smaller and the World Economy Bigger.* Princeton: Princeton University Press, 2016.

Lightner, Mikah and Matt O'Mara. *The Banana Trade War.* August 2013. http://www.stanford.edu/class/e297c/trade_environment/ wheeling/hbanana.html.

Maraniss, David, and Michael Weisskopf. "In Arkansas, the Game Is Chicken." *The Washington Post.* March 22, 1992. https://www. washingtonpost.com/archive/politics/1992/03/22/in-arkansas-the-game-is-chicken/6244e0fa-5416-4a6a-bae8-a229b854ed98/.

McKay, Betsy. "How a Russian Firm Decided Business Is the Same All over." *The Wall Street Journal.* September 15, 1997. https://www. wsj.com/articles/SB874274171751968500.

Nicks, Denver. "Who Actually Created Buffalo Wings?" *The Daily Beast.* September 28, 2016. https://www.thedailybeast.com/who-actually-created-buffalo-wings.

Ottaway, David B., and Dan B. Morgan. "For DNC Donor, 'Resistance' Was Overcome." *The Washington Post.* September 09, 1997. https://www.washingtonpost.com/wp-srv/politics/special/ campfin/stories/cf090997.htm.

Ottaway, David B., and Dan B. Morgan. "Gas Pipeline Bounces between Agendas." *The Washington Post.* October 05, 1998. https:// www.washingtonpost.com/wp-srv/inatl/europe/caspian100598.htm.

Pescatore, Tony, Steve Skelton, and Jacquie Jacob. *Processing Chickens*. University of Kentucky. College of Agriculture, Food and Environment. Lexington: ASC-210, 2013.

Rasizade, Alec. "The Mythology of Munificent Caspian Bonanza and Its Concomitant Pipeline Geopolitics." *Central Asia and the Caucasus Press*. AB. https://www.ca-c.org/journal/2001/journal_eng/cac-04/02.rasen.shtml.

Rasizade, Alec. "Azerbaijan and the Oil Trade: Prospects and Pitfalls." *The Brown Journal of World Affairs*, Summer/Fall 1997. http://bjwa.brown.edu/4-2/azerbaijan-and-the-oil-trade-prospects-and-pitfalls/.

Starr, Frederick S., and Svante E. Cornell. *The Baku-Tbilisi-Ceyhan Pipeline: Oil Window to the West*. Uppsala: Silk Road Studies Program, Uppsala University, 2005.

Suddath, Claire. "A Brief History of Buffalo Wings." *Time*. September 03, 2009. https://time.com/3957370/buffalo-wings/.

Sutela, Pekka. *Privatization in the Countries of Eastern and Central Europe and of the Former Soviet Union*. The United Nations University. World Institute for Development Economics Research. February 1998. https://www.wider.unu.edu/sites/default/files/wp146.pdf.

Tache, Ileana. "The Mass Privatization Process in Romania: A Case of Failed Anglo-Saxon Capitalism." *Metalurgia International 14*. (2010).

"Timeline of the Baku-Tbilisi-Ceyhan Pipeline." *Hurriyet Daily News*, July 13, 2006. https://web.archive.org/web/20161024173903/http://www.hurriyetdailynews.com/timeline-of-the-baku-tbilisi-ceyhan-pipeline.aspx?pageID=438&n=timeline-of-the-baku-tbilisi-ceyhan-pipeline-2006-07-13.

Tyrrell, James. "Feeding the World: Is Fish Better than Chicken?" *Physics World*. May 17, 2018. https://physicsworld.com/a/feeding-the-world-is-fish-better-than-chicken.

U.S. Congress. Committee on Governmental Affairs. *Investigation of Illegal or Improper Activities in Connection with 1996 Federal Election Campaigns: Final Report of the Committee on Governmental Affairs, United States Senate, Together with Additional and Minority Views.* Cong. Washington: U.S. G.P.O., 1998.

World Trade Organization. Committee on Sanitary and Phytosanitary Measures. *Summary of the Meeting Held on 14-15 March 2001.* Geneva: G/SPS/R/21, 2001.

World Trade Organization. Committee on Sanitary and Phytosanitary Measures. *Turkish SPS Measures Applied to Importation of Bananas.* Geneva: G/SPS/GEN/275, 24 August 2001.

World Trade Organization. Committee on Sanitary and Phytosanitary Measures. *Summary of the Meeting Held on 10-11 July 2001.* Geneva: G/SPS/R/22, 2001.

World Trade Organization. Committee on Sanitary and Phytosanitary Measures. *Summary of the Meeting Held on 22-23 June 2004.* Geneva: G/SPS/R/34, 2004.

"WTO Backs US in Banana Trade War." *BBC News.* February 08, 2008. http://news.bbc.co.uk/2/hi/business/7235191.stm.

INDEX

A NOTE ABOUT THE AUTHOR

Ahmad Ghannoum is a partner at Meirc Training & Consulting, where he leads the Procurement and Supply Chain Management practice and has trained over 6,000 industry professionals. He previously founded Hilltop Foods—a fresh fruit sourcing company—and has led corporate supply chain divisions in Turkey and Guinea as well as operated in a management consulting capacity over his 20-year career. He is a Fellow of the Chartered Institute of Logistics and Transport and an APICS Certified Supply Chain Professional. His enduring ambition has been to make sense of the world of supply, the lifeline of everything around us. He lives in Dubai, UAE, with his wife and two children.

Made in the USA
Coppell, TX
18 February 2022

73688421R00125